Interactions Access

Grammar

4th Edition

Patricia K. Werner

John P. Nelson

Marilynn Spaventa

 McGraw-Hill Contemporary

McGraw-Hill/Contemporary

*A Division of The **McGraw-Hill** Companies*

Interactions Access Grammar, 4th Edition

Published by McGraw-Hill/Contemporary, a business unit of The McGraw-Hill Companies, Inc., 1221 Avenue of the Americas, New York, NY 10020. Copyright © 2002, 1997, 1993 by The McGraw-Hill Companies, Inc. All rights reserved. No part of this publication may be reproduced or distributed in any form or by any means, or stored in a database or retrieval system, without the prior written consent of The McGraw-Hill Companies, Inc., including, but not limited to, in any network or other electronic storage or transmission, or broadcast for distance learning.

Some ancillaries, including electronic and print components, may not be available to customers outside the United States.

 This book is printed on recycled, acid-free paper containing 10% postconsumer waste.

2 3 4 5 6 7 8 9 0 QPD/QPD 0 9 8 7 6 5 4 3 2 1

ISBN 0-07-232982-3
ISBN 0-07-112402-0 (ISE)

Editorial director: *Tina B. Carver*
Series editor: *Annie Sullivan*
Developmental editor: *Jennifer Monaghan*
Director of marketing and sales: *Thomas P. Dare*
Project manager: *Joyce M. Berendes*
Production supervisor: *Kara Kudronowicz*
Coordinators of freelance design: *Michelle M. Meerclink/David W. Hash*
Interior designer: *Michael Warrell, Design Solutions*
Senior photo research coordinator: *Lori Hancock*
Photo research: *Pam Carley/Sound Reach*
Supplement coordinator: *Genevieve Kelley*
Compositor: *Interactive Composition Corporation*
Typeface: *10.5/12 Times Roman*
Printer: *Quebecor World Dubuque, IA*

Photo Credits: Chapter 1 Opener: © John Neubauer/PhotoEdit; p. 2: © Myrleen Cate/PhotoEdit; p. 22: © Malyszko/Stock, Boston; p. 24: © Karen Preuss/Image Works; **Chapter 2** Opener: © Michael Siluk/The Image Works; p. 39: © Latin Focus; p. 49: © Peter Menzel/Stock, Boston; **Chapter 3** Opener: © Michael Newman/PhotoEdit; p. 61: © Jean-Claude Lejeune; p. 73 (*left*): © Nancy Richmond/Image Works; (*right*): © Joel Gordon; p. 78 (*top*): © Joel Gordon; (*middle*): © Latin Focus; (*bottom*): © David J. Sams/Stock, Boston; **Chapter 4** Opener: © Elizabeth Crews/Stock, Boston; **Chapter 5** Opener: © D. Young-Wolff/PhotoEdit; p. 108 (*left*): © Judy Gelles/Stock, Boston; (*right*): © Bill Bachman/Photo Researchers; p. 113 © Bettmann/CORBIS; p. 117 (*left*): Courtesy Lawrence Zukof; (*right*): Courtesy Katharine Margaret Coe; p. 119: © Stock, Boston; p. 128 © Michael Newman/PhotoEdit; **Chapter 6** Opener: © Joel Gordon; p. 136 (*left*): © Bettmann/CORBIS; (*right*): © Bettmann/CORBIS; p. 145: © Elizabeth Crews/Stock, Boston; **Chapter 7** Opener: © Jeff Greenberg/PhotoEdit; **Chapter 8** Opener: © PhotoDisc Website; p. 189 (*left*): © Tom Cheek/Stock, Boston; (*right*): © Tony Freeman/PhotoEdit; p. 197 (*left*): © David Young-Wolff/PhotoEdit; (*right*): © Esbin Anderson/The Image Works; **Chapter 9** Opener: © PhotoDisc Website; p. 224 (both): Associated Press; **Chapter 10** Opener: © PhotoDisc Website; p. 235 (*left*): © Reinstein/The Image Works; (*center*): © Bill Bachman/The Image Works; (*right*): © Philippe Gontier/The Image Works; p. 241 (*left*): © Barbara Alper/Stock, Boston; (*right*): Associated Press/AP; p. 245: Associated Press/AP; p. 247: Hulton/Archive; p. 248 (*top left*): © Peter Menzel/Stock, Boston; (*top right*): © Bettmann/CORBIS; (*bottom left*): © Victor Englebert/Photo Researchers; (*bottom right*): Associated Press/AP.

INTERNATIONAL EDITION ISBN 0-07-112402-0
Copyright © 2002. Exclusive rights by The McGraw-Hill Companies, Inc. for manufacture and export. This book cannot be re-exported from the country to which it is sold by McGraw-Hill. The International Edition is not available in North America.

www.mhcontemporary.com/interactionsmosaic

Interactions Access **Grammar**

Boost your students' academic success!

Interactions Mosaic, 4th edition is the newly revised five-level, four-skill comprehensive ESL/EFL series designed to prepare students for academic content. The themes are integrated across proficiency levels and the levels are articulated across skill strands. The series combines communicative activities with skill-building exercises to boost students' academic success.

Interactions Mosaic, 4th edition features

- updated content
- five videos of authentic news broadcasts
- expansion opportunities through the Website
- new audio programs for the listening/speaking and reading books
- an appealing fresh design
- user-friendly instructor's manuals with placement tests and chapter quizzes

In This Chapter shows students the grammar points that will be covered in the chapter.

Chapter 2

Shopping and E-commerce

IN THIS CHAPTER

Part 1 The Present Continuous Tense: Affirmative Statements and Questions; *And; Too*

Part 2 Spelling Rules; Negative Statements; Using *But*

Part 3 More Prepositions of Place; *There is / There are* + subject + verb + *-ing; It* Versus *There*

Part 4 *To* and *To the* with Locations; *Because*

Setting the Context activities introduce key vocabulary and familiarize students with the chapter theme. Introductory activities include model conversations, readings, class discussions, prediction activities, previewing, and pair interviews.

Prereading Questions encourage students to share what they know about the topic before they read.

Check Your Understanding questions reinforce students' understanding of the topics through comprehension questions and encourage students to express themselves.

Grammar explanations and charts provide clear, easy to understand, and visually appealing grammar presentations.

Culture Notes offer interesting cultural insights related to the chapter theme.

Sample page 22:

22 Interactions Access Grammar

PART 4

There is / There are; Prepositions of Place; *At* and *At the* with Locations

Setting the Context

Prereading Questions This is a map of a region in the United States called New England. What states are in New England? What is the major city in New England?

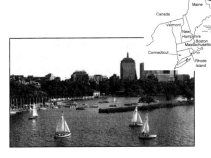

Canada
Maine
Vermont
New Hampshire
Boston
Massachusetts
Connecticut
Rhode Island

Boston

Boston is a beautiful city on the East Coast of the United States. It is the capital of Massachusetts, one of the states in New England. Boston is an old city, and there are many historic buildings, monuments, and churches. The State House (Massachusetts's capitol), Old City Hall, the King's Chapel, and Faneuil Hall are all downtown. Nearby there are also many interesting neighborhoods to visit, such as the North End, Beacon Hill, and Chinatown. Also, there are many lovely parks on the Charles River and along Boston Harbor. 5

Check Your Understanding Circle T for *True* or F for *False.*

1. T F Boston is on the West Coast of the United States.
2. T F Boston is the capital of New Jersey.

Sample page 111:

Chapter 5 Men and Women **111**

C. Information Questions with Who

	Examples	**Notes**
Statement	Catherine's parents were from Spain.	
Yes / No Question	*Was* or *were* + **subject** **Were** Catherine's parents from Spain?	
Question with *Who*	*Who* + *was* + **adjective, noun,** or **phrase.** **Who was** from Spain?	Questions with *who* are normally singular.

D. Information Questions with When, Where, How long, *and* How old

	Examples	**Possible Answers**
Statement	They were married in New York in 1941.	
Yes / No Question	*Was* or *were* + **subject** **Were** they married in New York in 1941?	Yes, they were.
Information Question	*Question word* + *was* or *were* + **subject** **When were** they married? **Where were** they married?	They were married in 1941. They were married in New York.

4 Make questions from these statements. The answers to the questions are the underlined words.

Examples: <u>Robert</u> was a medical student.
Who was a medical student?
They were introduced in <u>1938</u>.
When were they introduced?

1. Robert and Catherine were <u>at a dance</u>.
2. Robert was from <u>Philadelphia</u>.
3. <u>Catherine</u> was from New York.
4. She was <u>seventeen</u>.
5. He was <u>twenty-two</u>.
6. <u>Robert's parents</u> were Scandinavian.
7. Her family was from <u>Spain</u>.
8. They were married in <u>1941</u>.

  Marriage between people of different religions or cultural backgrounds was once unusual. Today, such marriages are much more common.

meat, (much/some) potatoes, and (a few/a little) vegetables. Today Americans   15
                                        14   15
aren't eating as (many/much) meat as in the past. They are adding (some/any)
                        16   17
beans and tofu to their meals. They are also trying to eat (a few/a little) fruit or
                                                                    18
(a few/a little) vegetables at every meal. But Americans still eat (a lot of/many)
          19   20
junk food too.

Using What You've Learned

4 Discussing Diets.   Discuss these questions in a small group. Then choose one student to tell the class about the discussion.

1. What was the traditional diet of your parents or grandparents?
2. How is your diet changing?
3. What is your opinion about these changes?

5 Discussing World Records.   Read the following information from *Guinness World Records 2000*, Bantam Books, by Guinness Publishing Ltd. pages 92 to 94.

Largest Sushi Roll   Six hundred members of the Nikopoka Festa committee made a sushi roll (kappamaki) that was 3,279 ft. long at Yoshii, Japan, on October 12, 1997.

Biggest Restaurant Steak   A 12 lb.8oz. rump steak (precooked weight) is available at the Kestrel Inn, Hatton, England. It takes about 40 minutes to cook and costs $128. If a customer finishes the steak, the management will make a donation to charity.

Biggest Bowl of Spaghetti   On August 16, 1998, a bowl of spaghetti weighing 605 lbs. was cooked by Consolidated Communication in London, England, on behalf of Disney Home Video to celebrate the rerelease of the movie, Lady and the Tramp.

Biggest Hamburger   The biggest hamburger ever weighed 2.5 tons and was made at the Outagimie County Fairgrounds in Seymour, Wisconsin, on August 5, 1989.

Biggest Ice Cream Sundae   On July 24, 1988, the biggest ice cream sundae ever, weighing 22.59 tons, was put together by Palm Dairies Ltd. Alberta, Canada. The finished concoction included 18.38 tons of ice cream, 3.98 tons of syrup, and 537 lb.3oz. of topping.

Make four questions for your partner to answer.

Examples: *How long was the largest sushi roll? Who made the largest sushi roll?*

- Ask your partner questions and answer your partner's questions.
- Look in the library or on the Internet for more world food records to tell your

---

Using What You've Learned sections provide students with opportunities to do less structured, more communicative activities.

Groupwork activities maximize opportunities for discussion.

Pairwork activities encourage students to personalize and practice the target language.

Checking Your Progress helps students review what they've learned and become familiar with standardized test formats.

Checking Your Progress

Check your progress with structures from Chapters 7 and 8. Be sure to review any problem areas.

Part 1.   Choose the correct word(s) to complete each sentence.

1. Antonietta _____ a wonderful idea while she was riding the bus.
   a. have
   b. has
   c. had
   d. having
   e. is having

2. When the doorbell rang, I _____ out of my seat.
   a. was jumping
   b. jump
   c. jumps
   d. jumped
   e. jumping

3. Students in a new school often need _____ advice.
   a. a lot of
   b. many
   c. a lot
   d. a few
   e. lots

4. There weren't _____ people in the classroom, so it was easy to find a good seat.
   a. much
   b. some
   c. a few
   d. many
   e. a lot

5. While Juan and Silvia _____ to class last night, they saw an accident.
   a. walking
   b. walked
   c. were walking
   d. walk
   e. are walking

6. Pablo didn't have _____ eggs, so he couldn't bake a cake.
   a. any
   b. a little
   c. much
   d. a lot
   e. some

7. While Duc was studying, the telephone _____ two times.
   a. rings
   b. is ringing
   c. was ringing
   d. ring
   e. rang

8. I don't have any money, but Jean has _____.
   a. much
   b. a lot of
   c. many
   d. a few
   e. some

9. When I turned on the computer, the electricity _____ out.
   a. go
   b. went
   c. is going
   d. was going
   e. was gone

10. Mari's class has many international students, but my class has only _____.
    a. a lot
    b. a lot of
    c. a little
    d. any
    e. a few

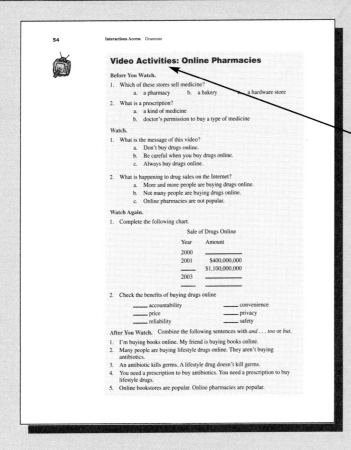

Video Activities: Online Pharmacies

Before You Watch.

1. Which of these stores sell medicine?
   a. a pharmacy   b. a bakery   c. a hardware store

2. What is a prescription?
   a. a kind of medicine
   b. doctor's permission to buy a type of medicine

Watch.

1. What is the message of this video?
   a. Don't buy drugs online.
   b. Be careful when you buy drugs online.
   c. Always buy drugs online.

2. What is happening to drug sales on the Internet?
   a. More and more people are buying drugs online.
   b. Not many people are buying drugs online.
   c. Online pharmacies are not popular.

Watch Again.

1. Complete the following chart.

Sale of Drugs Online

Year	Amount
2000	_____
2001	$400,000,000
_____	$1,100,000,000
2003	_____
_____	_____

2. Check the benefits of buying drugs online

   _____ accountability   _____ convenience
   _____ price   _____ privacy
   _____ reliability   _____ safety

After You Watch.   Combine the following sentences with *and . . . too* or *but*.

1. I'm buying books online. My friend is buying books online.
2. Many people are buying lifestyle drugs online. They aren't buying antibiotics.
3. An antibiotic kills germs. A lifestyle drug doesn't kill germs.
4. You need a prescription to buy antibiotics. You need a prescription to buy lifestyle drugs.
5. Online bookstores are popular. Online pharmacies are popular.

Video news broadcasts immerse students in authentic language, complete with scaffolding and follow-up activities.

Don't forget to check out the new *Interactions Mosaic* Website at www.mhcontemporary.com/interactionsmosaic.

- ■ Traditional practice and interactive activities
- ■ Links to student and teacher resources
- ■ Cultural activities
- ■ Focus on Testing
- ■ Activities from the Website are also provided on CD-ROM

Interactions Access — Grammar Scope and Sequence

Chapter 1

Neighborhoods, Cities, and Towns

PART 1

The Verb *Be:* Affirmative Statements; Contractions; Questions

Setting the Context

Prereading Questions   Look at the photo. Look at the title of the reading. Where is the young woman? Is she happy?

Lost in New York City!

Hi! I'm Mariko. I'm from Japan. I'm Japanese. I'm an exchange student in San Diego. Right now I'm in New York on a special tour. My tour group is at the United Nations building. But where is the United Nations building? I'm lost! New York is a very big city. I'm confused, and I'm nervous. Where are my friends?

Check Your Understanding   Circle T for *True* or F for *False*.

Example: T Ⓕ Her name is Tomoko.

1. T F Mariko is from Japan.
2. T F Mariko is in San Diego right now.
3. T F Mariko is a businesswoman.
4. T F Mariko is lost.

A. Affirmative Statements

Form	Subject + *be* + adjective, noun, or phrase	
Singular		**Plural**
I **am** Japanese. You **are** students. He She } **is** in New York. It		We **are** Japanese. You **are** students. They **are** in New York.
Expressions		**Examples**
Be from (place) **Be in (place)**		I **am from** New York. She **is from** Athens. We **are in** California now. They **are in** the library.

1 Use *am, is,* or *are* to complete this reading. The first one is done as an example.

I __am__ Mariko, and I _____ an exchange student in San Diego. This week
                          1

I _____ in New York. I _____ on a trip with people from my school. Today my
       2   3

friends and I _____ on a city tour. My friends _____ from many places. Anne _____
              4   5   6

French. She _____ from Paris. Hassan _____ from Syria, and Carlos and Gabriel
            7   8

_____ from Mexico. We _____ excited but nervous! New York _____ very large,
9   10   11

and it _____ crowded.
       12

2 Use *am, is,* or *are* and a nationality to complete these sentences. Look at page 4, Activity 3, for nationalities.

1. Mariko __is__ from Japan. She __is Japanese.__

2. Carlos _____ from Mexico. He _____ _____.

3. Mr. Kim and Mr. Park _____ from Korea. They _____ _____.

4. Anne and Chantal _____ from France. They _____ _____.

5. Hassan _____ from Syria. He _____ _____.

6. Benny _____ from Indonesia. He _____ _____.

7. Gunter and Elizabeth _____ from Germany. They _____ _____.

8. Chun is from Taiwan. She _____ _____.

9. Carolina and Andre _____ from Brazil. They _____ _____.

10. I _____ from _____. I _____ _____.

3   Use the correct form of the verb *be* and *she, he,* or *they* to complete these sentences.

1. Mariko ___*is*___ from Japan. ___*She*___ ___*is*___ Japanese.

2. Elizabeth _____ from Germany. _____ _____ German.

3. Benny _____ from Indonesia. _____ _____ Indonesian.

4. Carlos and Gabriel are from Mexico. _____ _____ Mexican.

5. Anne is from France. _____ _____ French.

6. Mr. Park _____ from Korea. _____ _____ Korean.

7. Hassan and Ali _____ from Syria. _____ _____ Syrian.

8. Chun _____ from Taiwan. _____ _____ Taiwanese.

9. Carolina and Andre _____ from Brazil. _____ _____ Brazilian.

4   Use *I* or *we* to complete this conversation.

Lucy: Good morning, everyone. __I__ am Lucy Moore. _____ am from New York. _____
                                                                1   2
am happy to welcome you to my city.

Bruce: Hi. _____ am Bruce Moore. _____ am from California, but New York is my city
            3   4
now! _____ are your tour guides, and _____ are very happy to be here today.
    5   6

Lucy: _____ are ready to start. Today _____ are in Manhattan, the heart of New York
       7   8
City.

B. Contractions

Singular	Plural	Long Form	
I**'m** from Spain.	We**'re** from Spain.	I **am**	We **are**
You**'re** from Korea.	You**'re** from Korea.	You **are**	You **are**
He**'s** } She**'s** } from Brazil. It**'s** }	They**'re** from Brazil.	He } She } **is** It }	They **are**

Note: People often use contractions in conversation. Contractions are sometimes used with names: *Anne's from France; Hassan's from Syria.*

5   Read this paragraph. Then write it again with contractions.

Example: *Hi, I'm Carlos . . .*

Hi! I am Carlos, and I am from Mexico. I am a student in Chicago, but I am in New York on a tour. My brother Gabriel is here in New York too. He is on vacation. We are very excited about our trip. New York is wonderful! It is big, crowded, and interesting. Some people on our tour are afraid of the city. They are nervous—especially Mariko. She is very nice, but she is always lost and confused. Not Gabriel and me! We are in love with New York!   5

C. Yes/No Questions

Form	*Be* + subject + adjective, noun, or phrase	
	Singular	**Plural**
Am I happy?		**Are** we happy?
Are you nervous?		**Are** you nervous?
Is { he she it } lost?		**Are** they lost?

6   Work with a partner. Ask and answer these questions. Answer using Yes or No.

Example: A.   Is Mariko Japanese?
              B.   Yes.
              A.   Is Carlos Japanese?
              B.   No.

1.   Is Mariko in New York City now?
2.   Is she from Hong Kong?
3.   Is she an exchange student?
4.   Are Carlos and Gabriel from Argentina?
5.   Is Gabriel on vacation?
6.   Are Carlos and Gabriel in love with New York City?
7.   Are you from Japan?
8.   Are you in New York now?
9.   Is your teacher happy?
10.   Are you nervous?

D. Questions with How, Where, and Who

Form	Question word + *be* + subject	
	Questions	**Possible Answers**
How		
Greetings	**How are** you?	Fine, thank you.
Age	**How old** is he?	Twenty-five.
Where		
Hometown or country	**Where** are you from?	I am from Turkey.
Location	**Where** are you?	I'm in New York.
Who		
Identity	**Who** is your roommate?	My roommate is Mariko.

7   Write a question for each answer. Use *How, Where,* and *Who* in your questions. Then work with a partner. Take turns asking and answering the questions. The first one is done as an example.

1.   *How are you?*

I'm fine, thanks, but I'm a little homesick.

2.   _____ ?

I'm from France.

3.   _____ ?

I'm twenty-five.

4.   _____ ?

My friend is Chantal.

5.   _____ ?

She's from France too.

6.   _____ ?

She's at the hotel right now.

E. The Verb Be with Adjectives

Form	Subject + *be* + adjective	
Singular		**Plural**
I'**m** tired. You'**re** happy. He'**s** She'**s** } **lost.** It'**s**		We'**re** tired. You'**re** happy. They'**re** lost.
Expressions		**Examples**
Be new here **Be new to (place)**		I **am new** here. They **are new to** New York.

8 There are good things and bad things about New York City. Make sentences about the city. Use the pictures and the vocabulary to help you. Make one sentence for each adjective.

Example: *Parts of New York City are clean.*

1. Parts of New York City are _____.
    beautiful
    ✓clean
    safe

2. Parts of New York City are _____.
    ugly
    dirty
    dangerous

3. Buildings in New York City are _____.
   large
   modern

4. Buildings in New York City are _____.
   small
   old

5. New York City is _____.
   crowded
   noisy

6. New York City is _____.
   peaceful
   clean

7. Some New Yorkers are _____.
   unhappy
   unfriendly

8. Some New Yorkers are _____.
   happy
   friendly

9   Choose a word to describe these people.

bored	✓homesick	thirsty
excited	hungry	tired

Example: Anne and Chantal are _homesick._

1. Mr. Park and Mr. Kim are _____.
2. Benny is _____.
3. Carlos and Gabriel are _____.
4. Hassan is _____.
5. Gunter and Elizabeth are _____.

F. Questions with What and What . . . Like

Form	What + *be* + subject	
	Questions	**Possible Answers**
Names	**What** is your (first) name?	Mariko.
	What is your last (family) name?	It's Kanno.
Languages	**What** is Mariko's first (native) language?	Japanese.

Form	What + *be* + subject + like	
	Questions	**Possible Answers**
Descriptions	**What** is Mariko like?	She's nice.
	What is New York like?	It's big and crowded.

10 Ask and answer questions with *What . . . like?* Use the cues to talk about these cities.

Example: Tokyo / big and crowded
    A.   What is Tokyo like?
    B.   It's big and crowded.

1.   New York / large and very busy
2.   San Francisco / beautiful
3.   Cairo / crowded but very interesting
4.   Los Angeles / modern but polluted
5.   Rome / old and beautiful but very expensive
6.   Minneapolis / safe and clean
7.   Rio de Janeiro / fun
8.   Paris / beautiful and interesting

Using What You've Learned

11 **Introducing Your Classmates.**

■   Stand up and make a line. Make the line in alphabetical order by your first name. **Example:** Alberto, Beat, Carolina, etc.
■   Each person says his or her name. Is the alphabetical order correct?
■   Can you remember everyone's name? Each person says all of the names and his or her own. **Example:** Alberto, Beat, Carolina. I'm Edward.

Repeat the names and this time also say the city or town you are from. Alberto is from Mexico City. Beat is from Basil. Carolina is from Vera Cruz. I'm from Mexico City.

12 **Telling About Yourself.**   Use the paragraph in Activity 5 on page 5 as a model. Write a paragraph about yourself, your city, and your friends or classmates.

13 **Telling Stories.**   Change your name. Change your age. Create a new person!

■ Write your new name, age, hometown, country, and language on a piece of paper.

> **Example:** *Stella Blanco, 28, Buenos Aires, Argentina, Spanish*
>
> or
>
> *William Shakespeare, 200+, Stratford, England, English*

■ Then work in small groups. Ask other students questions, and write the information in a chart like the one below. Here are some questions: Who are you? How old are you? Where are you from? What is your native language? Finally, introduce your "new" friends.

> **Example:** *This is my "new" friend, Stella Blanco. She is 28 years old. She is from Buenos Aires, Argentina, and she speaks Spanish.*

Name	Age	Hometown/Country	Language
Stella Blanco	28	Buenos Aires, Argentina	Spanish
William Shakespeare	200+	Stratford, England	English

14 **Learning About Students in Your Class.**   Ask and answer questions about your hometown or city. Write your information in the chart. Then take turns telling the class about the other students. Some questions:

■ What is your hometown?

■ What is your hometown like?

■ Is it safe (beautiful, clean, expensive etc.)?

Example: *Marco is from Brazil. He comes from Sao Paulo.*

Name	Hometown/Country	Description of Hometown

PART 2

Nouns; Spelling Rules; Negative Statements; Possessive Adjectives

Setting the Context

Prereading Questions   Look at the picture. Where are these people? Is their home near a large city?

Life in a Small Town

My name is Gary, and I'm a farmer. My hometown is Belleville, Wisconsin. It's a small town with a population of about 1,800. It's not a busy, crowded place. It's very quiet and peaceful. The streets are safe, and the people are friendly. It's not dangerous   5
here. Our air is not polluted. It's very clean. I'm happy in Belleville, and my family is very happy here too. Our dream is a good future in Belleville.

Check Your Understanding   Complete these sentences.

1. His name is ————————————.

2. He is a ————————————.

3. Belleville is a ———————————— town.

4. Gary and his family are ———————————— in Belleville.

In 1900, about ten million people in the United States lived on farms. Today, only about four million people live on farms. What are some possible reasons for this change?

A. Nouns

Singular		
Consonant Sound	**Vowel Sound**	**Notes**
I am **a doctor.** Are you **a student?** Juan is **a citizen.**	I am **an engineer.** Are you **an exchange student?** Juan is **an immigrant.**	Use *a* or *an* with a singular noun. Use *a* before a consonant sound. Use *an* before a vowel sound.

Plural		
Consonant Sound	**Vowel Sound**	**Notes**
We are **doctors.** Are you **students?** They are **citizens.**	We are **engineers.** Are you **exchange students?** They are **immigrants.**	Do not use *a* or *an* with plural nouns.

1   Here are names of some occupations. Number them in alphabetical order. Then add *a* or *an* before each occupation.

_____ _____ nurse's aide   _____ _____ musician

_____ _____ plumber   _____ _____ dentist

__1__ __an__ airplane pilot   _____ _____ student

_____ _____ computer programmer   _____ _____ engineer

_____ _____ nurse   _____ _____ bus driver

_____ _____ carpenter   _____ _____ secretary

_____ _____ English teacher   _____ _____ doctor

_____ _____ businesswoman   _____ _____ auto mechanic

2   Talk about these people. Follow the examples and make complete sentences. Add *a* or *an* when necessary.

Examples: *Hau is from Vietnam.*   *Ali and Mohammed are from Jordan.*
               He is a musician.   *They are carpenters.*

1. Soo Young   2. Alfonso   3. Andrea   4. Nancy
    Korea   Colombia   Argentina   the United States
    student   engineer   doctor   flight attendant

5. Centa and
   Werner
   Switzerland
   teachers

6. Tomoko and
   Akiko
   Japan
   computer
   programmers

7. Isabelle and
   Pierre
   France
   factory workers

8. Daniel and Ben
   Hong Kong
   auto mechanics

B. Spelling Rules for Nouns

Notes	Singular	Plural
Most plural nouns end in -s	friend student teacher	friends students teachers
Nouns ending with consonant + y change to -ies	city family party	cities families parties
Nouns ending with vowel + y add -s only	boy key play	boys keys plays
Nouns ending with ch, sh, s, and x add -es	church dish kiss box	churches dishes kisses boxes
Nouns ending with consonant + o add -es	potato tomato	potatoes tomatoes
Nouns ending with vowel + o add -s only	radio zoo	radios zoos
Nouns ending with f or fe change to -ves	shelf wife	shelves wives
Some irregular nouns	person child man woman foot goose mouse	people children men women feet geese mice

3   Write the plurals of these nouns.

Example: child _____ *children* _____   dish _____ *dishes* _____

1. man _____
2. woman _____
3. baby _____
4. boy _____
5. church _____

6. potato _____
7. toy _____
8. farm _____
9. city _____
10. wife _____

4   Use plural nouns to complete the reading.

Our _farms_ (farm) are busy _____ (place). There are many _____
1   2
(animal) to take care of. We have _____ (cow), _____ (horse),
3   4
_____ (chicken), _____ (duck), and _____ (goose). Our
5   6   7
_____ (child) have many _____ (pet): _____ (dog), _____
8   9   10   11
(cat), and even _____ (mouse)! Both our _____ (wife) have big
12   13
_____ (garden) too. There are _____ (flower) and _____ (veg-
14   15   16
etable) to take care of. Right now we have _____ (carrot), _____ (onion),
17   18
_____ (tomato), and _____ (potato). There are many, many _____
19   20   21
(thing) to do. Our _____ (family) are always busy on the farm.
22

> Wheat, apples, and corn are three important products of farms in North America.
> What are some other important farm products that you know?

C. Negative Statements

Form	Subject + *be* + not	
Long Form	**Contraction**	**Contraction**
I **am not** late.	I**'m not** late.	(No contraction)
You **are not** late.	You**'re not** late.	You **aren't** late.
He She **is not** late. It	He**'s** She**'s** **not** late. It**'s**	He She **isn't** late. It
We You **are not** late. They	We**'re** You**'re** **not** late. They**'re**	We You **aren't** late. They

5   Complete these sentences with the correct negative form of the verb *be*. Use
contractions.

1.   The buses here _____ fast. In fact, they're very slow.

2.   My town _____ large. In fact, it's very small.

3.   My town _____ ugly. In fact, it's very pretty.

4.   My neighborhood _____ dangerous. In fact, it's very safe.

5. Our neighbors _____ shy people. In fact, they're very friendly.

6. I _____ bored here. In fact, I'm very busy and happy.

7. You _____ a stranger here. In fact, you're a part of the family!

8. He _____ a student. In fact, he's a teacher.

6 These sentences are not true. To make them true, change them to the negative. Give all possible forms.

Example: Denver is a small city.

Denver is not a small city.
Denver's not a small city.
Denver isn't a small city.

1. Gary is a businessman.
2. He's from a large city.
3. The White House is in New York.
4. It's near the United Nations building.
5. New York is a quiet city.
6. It is near Los Angeles.
7. You are from England.
8. I am tired of grammar.

7 Use *am, is,* or *are* to complete these sentences. Use a contraction form when possible. Use negative forms when you see (not).

1. I'_m_ from Victoria, British Columbia. It _____ (not) a big city, but it
   ₁

   _____ (not) a small town either. It _____ (not) on the mainland. It
   ₂   ₃

   _____ on Vancouver Island. Victoria _____ very beautiful. The weather
   ₄   ₅

   _____ often warm and sunny, but it _____ sometimes rainy.
   ₆   ₇

2. We _____ from Marlboro, Vermont, and we _____ very happy here.
   ₁   ₂

   Marlboro _____ (not) very big, so it _____ (not) noisy or crowded. Our
   ₃   ₄

   streets _____ (not) dangerous or dirty. Our neighbors _____ friendly, and our
   ₅   ₆

   little town _____ very nice.
   ₇

3. Hi! My name _____ Natalie. I _____ twenty-two. I _____ from
   ₁   ₂   ₃

   Switzerland, but I _____ (not) there now. I _____ in Houston. Houston
   ₄   ₅

   _____ huge. It _____ (not) a quiet city, but it _____ interesting.
   ₆   ₇   ₈

D. Possessive Adjectives

Singular	
I am Natalie.	**My** name is Natalie.
You are Nancy.	**Your** name is Nancy.
He is Hau.	**His** name is Hau.
She is Mei.	**Her** name is Mei.
It is Lukas (the dog).	**Its** name is Lukas (the dog).

Plural	
We are Ali and Mohammed.	**Our** names are Ali and Mohammed.
You are Isabelle and Pierre.	**Your** names are Isabelle and Pierre.
They are Daniel and Ben.	**Their** names are Daniel and Ben.

8   Circle the correct form.

1. (I / (My)) name is Natalie.
2. (I / My) am from Switzerland.
3. (We / Our) hometown is Berne.
4. (We / Our) are from Switzerland.
5. (I / My) family is in Switzerland now.
6. What is (you / your) name?
7. How old are (you / your)?
8. (He / His) name is Gary.
9. (She / Her) is Nancy.
10. (They / Their) dog is Lukas.
11. (It / Its) name is Lukas.
12. (It / Its) is seven years old.

9   Use *I, we, my,* or *our* to complete these sentences.

1. __We__ are from Big City, U.S.A. _____ city is very crowded. _____ air is pol-
       ₁   ₂

   luted, and _____ streets are dirty and dangerous. _____ lives are not easy here.
              ₃   ₄

   _____ aren't very happy in Big City. _____ dream is a home in the country.
   ₅   ₆

2. _____ am from Middletown, Canada. _____ city isn't big, but it isn't small
   ₁   ₂

   either. _____ life is peaceful and _____ am very happy. _____ neighbors are
           ₃   ₄   ₅

   friendly, and _____ neighborhood is safe.
                 ₆

10   Use *he, she, they, his, her,* or *their* to complete this reading.

Isabelle and Pierre are from France. ___*They*___ are factory workers. _____ jobs
₁
aren't very interesting, and _____ are often difficult. Isabelle's work is sometimes
₂
dangerous. _____ isn't happy with _____ job, and _____ dream is to study at
₃   ₄   ₅
the university someday. Pierre is happy with _____ job, but _____ is worried
₆   ₇
about Isabelle. _____ dream is to save money for Isabelle's education.
₈

Using What You've Learned

11   **Telling Stories.**   Write a story about a friend or a relative. Use these questions and the
ideas from Activities 9 and 10 to help you. Attach a photograph or drawing of your
friend to your story.

1.   Who is this person?
2.   Where is he or she from?
3.   What is that place like?
4.   What is the person's occupation?
5.   Is he or she happy?
6.   What are that person's dreams for the future?

PART 3

The Verb *Be* with Time and Weather

Setting the Context

Prereading Questions   Who is the woman in this picture? Is the weather nice today?

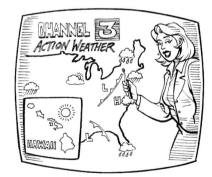

A Weather Forecast
    Good evening. Today is March 24, and
the weather is bad on the East Coast. Everywhere it's rainy, snowy, foggy, cloudy, or
windy! Right now, at 6:15, it's rainy in Miami.
It's foggy in Washington, D.C., and the airport   5
is closed. It's cold and windy in New York
City. In Montreal, it's snowy. The place to be
right now is Hawaii!

Check Your Understanding   Complete these sentences.

1.   It's March _____.

2.   In Miami, it's _____.

3. In Washington, it's _____.

4. The airport is _____.

5. In Montreal, it's _____.

In the United States, people use the Fahrenheit Scale for temperature. Most of the world uses the Centigrade Scale. On the Fahrenheit Scale, water freezes at 32°. To convert from Celsius to Fahrenheit, use this formula °Celsius = 5/9 (°F–32). Many Websites display temperatures in both scales.

A. Using It with Weather

Form	What + *be* + subject (+ like)	It + be + adjective
	Questions	**Possible Answers**
What's the weather today?		**It's** beautiful.
What's the weather **like?**		**It's** terrible.
What's it **like** out(side)?		**It's** nice.

1 Work with a partner. Make complete sentences about the weather in these cities. Use the weather maps to help you. Use the map on the left to answer questions 1–5 and the map on the right to answer questions 6–10.

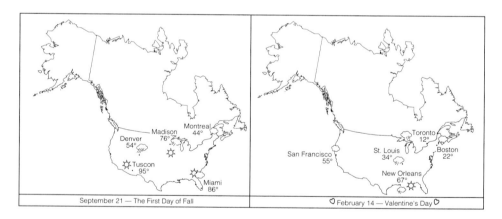

Example: New York / cloudy and cool

New York is cloudy and cool today.

1. Madison, Wisconsin / sunny, breezy, and warm
2. Denver, Colorado / cloudy, rainy, and cool
3. Miami, Florida / hot and humid
4. Montreal, Quebec / cold and cloudy
5. Tucson, Arizona / very hot and dry
6. Boston, Massachusetts / cold and snowy
7. New Orleans, Louisiana / warm and breezy

8. St. Louis, Missouri / cold and rainy
9. San Francisco, California / foggy and cool
10. Toronto, Ontario / very cold and windy

Many people talk about the weather to start a conversation. For example, they say, "Nice day, isn't it?" Or "Hot enough for you?" Or "It's very cold for this time of year." How do you start a conversation with people you don't well know?

B. Using It with Time

Form	What (+ noun) + be + it	It + be + time expression
	Questions	**Possible Answers**
What time is it?		It's eight o'clock.
		It's 8:20 P.M.
What day is it?		It's Friday.
What month is it?		It's August.
What's the date (today)?		It's August 20th.
What year is it?		It's 2002.

2 Work with a partner. Tell the time, day, or date.

Example: *It's 8:15.*

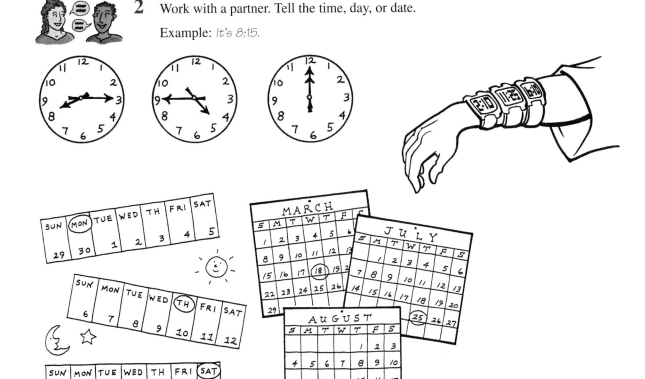

3 Work with a partner. Ask and answer these questions.

1. What time is it right now?
2. What day is it?
3. What's the date today?
4. What month is it?
5. What season is it? (winter, spring, summer, fall?)
6. What year is it?

C. Prepositions of Time—In, On, At, From . . . to (until)

	Period of Time	Examples
In	general time of day	Alex was born **in** the afternoon.
		Marina was born **in** the morning.
	month	Alex was born **in** July.
	season	Alex was born **in** the summer.
	year	Alex was born **in** 1986.
On	days	My birthday is **on** Saturday.
	dates	My birthday is **on** September 20th.
	also: weekdays	I go to school **on** weekdays.
	weekends	I'm at home **on** weekends.
At	specific times	My class is **at** 8:30 P.M.
	also: at night	The party is **at** night.
From . . . to (until)	beginning and ending times	The dinner is **from** 6:00 **to** 8:00.
		The party is **from** 8:30 **until** midnight.

Expressions with Birthdays	Examples
What day is your birthday?	It's (**on**) September 20th.
When were you born?	I was born **on** September 20th.

4 Use *on* or *at* to complete these sentences.

1. Martin was born ⎯*on*⎯ August 20th. He was born ⎯⎯ Friday ⎯⎯ 8:20 P.M.

2. Marina's birthday is ⎯⎯ December 23rd. She was born ⎯⎯ night.

3. Gary's birthday is ⎯⎯ April 26th. He was born ⎯⎯ midnight.

4. Alex's birthday is ⎯⎯ July 25th. He was born ⎯⎯ Thursday ⎯⎯ 5:25 P.M.

5. Jennifer's birthday is ⎯⎯ November 27th. She was born ⎯⎯ 6:30 P.M.

5 Circle the correct prepositions.

I'm usually awake (at/on) 6:15 A.M. (in/on) weekdays. I'm at work (from/at)
              1   2

8:00 (in/on) the morning. I work (at/from) 8:00 (in/to) 4:30 (at/in) the afternoon.
        3   4   5   6

Then I'm at school (in / from) 7:00 (on / to) 8:30 (at / in) night. (In / On) the weekends,
7   8   9   10

I'm very lazy. I'm still in bed (at / from) 10:00 A.M.
11

6 Fill out the following chart for your personal schedule on weekdays.

Activity	get up	eat breakfast	at school	eat lunch	study	go home	eat dinner	relax	go to bed
Time									

Talk about your schedule with your classmates.

Then write a short composition about yourself. Use the paragraph in Activity 5 on pages 20 to 21 as an example.

7 Use *in, on, from,* or *to* to complete this reading.

The weather in Wisconsin is very changeable. __*In*__ the spring, it's cool and rainy.

_____ the summer, it's often very hot. _____ the fall, the weather is lovely.
        1   2

Then, _____ November _____ April, it's cold and snowy. I'm always busy,
        3   4

good weather or bad weather. But _____ Sundays, I rest a little.
                                        5

8 Use *at, in, on, from,* or *to* to complete this reading.

My life in New York City is very busy. My home is far from my work, so __*from*__

Monday _____ Friday, I am awake _____ 5:00 _____ the morning.
        1   2   3

_____ Monday, Wednesday, and Friday, I take the bus to work. _____
        4   5

Tuesday and Thursday, I drive my car. My day is very long. I am usually home

_____ 7:30 or 8:00 P.M. _____ the weekend, I sleep late.
        6   7

Using What You've Learned

9 **Telling About the Weather.** Write two sentences about the weather in your city or town today. If you can use the Internet, look for the weather in five different cities you want to visit. Write sentences for each. If you can't use the Internet, write about five cities and use *probably* in your sentences.

Example: *Today it's sunny here. It's also windy and cool. In Bangkok, it's probably hot and humid. It's probably very cloudy.*

10 **Telling About Birthdays.** As a class, take turns telling about your birthday. Give the date. If you know, also say the day of the week and the time of day you were born. One student can write down all the birth dates.

| **PART 4** | # *There is / There are;* Prepositions of Place; *At* and *At the* with Locations |

Setting the Context

Prereading Questions   This is a map of a region in the United States called New England. What states are in New England? What is the major city in New England?

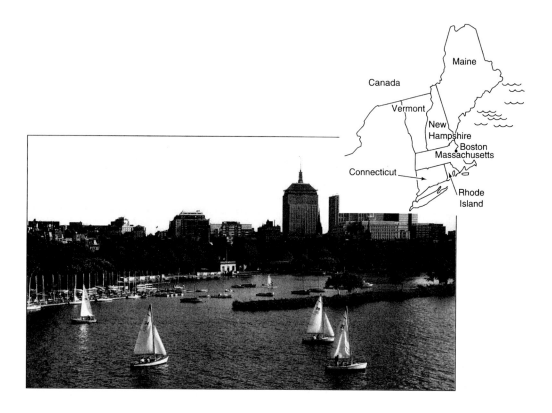

Boston

Boston is a beautiful city on the East Coast of the United States. It is the capital of Massachusetts, one of the states in New England. Boston is an old city, and there are many historic buildings, monuments, and churches. The State House (Massachusetts's capitol), Old City Hall, the King's Chapel, and Faneuil Hall are all downtown. Nearby there are also many interesting neighborhoods to visit, such as the North End, Beacon Hill, and Chinatown. Also, there are many lovely parks on the Charles River and along Boston Harbor.

5

Check Your Understanding   Circle T for *True* or F for *False.*

1.   T F Boston is on the West Coast of the United States.
2.   T F Boston is the capital of New Jersey.

3.   T   F   There are many historic buildings in Boston.
4.   T   F   There is a Chinese neighborhood in Boston.
5.   T   F   There aren't many parks in Boston.

Boston is a historic city in the United States. What historic places do you know? What are some interesting things to see there?

A. There is / There are—*Affirmative and Negative Statements*

Affirmative Statements

Form	There + *be* + subject	
	Long Form	**Contraction**
With a singular noun	**There is** a museum downtown.	**There's** a museum downtown.
With plural nouns	**There are** many banks downtown.	**There're** many banks downtown.

Negative Statements

Form	There + *be* + *not* + subject	
	Long Form	**Contraction**
With a singular noun	**There is not** a post office nearby.	**There isn't** a post office nearby.
With plural nouns	**There are not** many stores downtown.	**There aren't** many stores downtown.

1   Use *isn't* or *aren't* to complete these sentences.

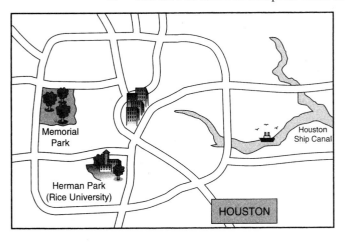

1.   There ___*isn't*___ a wharf in Houston.

2.   There _____ many large parks.

3.   There _____ many rivers.

4.   There _____ mountains nearby.

5.   There _____ many hills in Houston.

6.   There _____ cable cars.

7.   There _____ a subway.

8.   There _____ snow in Houston.

2   Use *is* or *are* to complete these sentences.

1.   There ___*is*___ a subway in San Francisco.

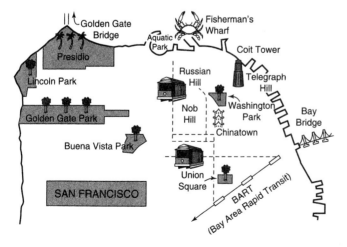

2. There _____ many parks in San Francisco.

3. There _____ many hills in San Francisco.

4. There _____ many cable cars.

5. There _____ a wharf for boats called Fisherman's Wharf.

6. There _____ a large Chinese neighborhood in San Francisco.

7. There _____ a tower in San Francisco.

8. There _____ many bridges.

B. There is /There are—*Questions and Short Answers*

Form	Be + *there* + subject			
	Questions		**Possible Answers**	
			Affirmative	**Negative**
Singular	**Is there** a post office nearby?		Yes, **there is.**	No, **there isn't.**
Plural	**Are there** many stores downtown?		Yes, **there are.**	No, **there aren't.**

3 Ask and answer questions. Use the cues to make questions. Use the map to help you.

Examples: many bridges to Manhattan
        A.   Are there many bridges to Manhattan?
        B.   Yes, there are.
        an island in the East River
        A.   Is there an island in the East River?
        B.   Yes, there is.

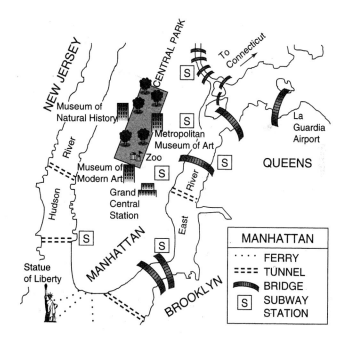

1.   a subway in Manhattan
2.   many tunnels
3.   four rivers around Manhattan
4.   a bridge to the Statue of Liberty
5.   many ferries to Manhattan
6.   a train station in Manhattan
7.   a large park
8.   a zoo in Central Park

9.   many museums in Manhattan
10. an airport in Manhattan
11. an airport in Brooklyn
12. an airport in Queens

C. The Verb Be with Prepositions of Place—In, On, At

Prepositions	Uses	Examples
In	buildings cities states regions countries	She lives **in** an apartment. Her apartment is **in** Boston. Boston is **in** Massachusetts. Massachusetts is **in** New England. New England is **in** the United States.
On	bodies of water and coasts (including the East Coast and the West Coast) streets	Boston is **on** the Charles River. Massachusetts is **on** the East Coast. Her apartment is **on** Beacon Street.
At	specific addresses and many specific locations	She lives **at** 121 Beacon Street. She works **at** the bank. Right now she is **at** the store. Her sister is **at** the library.

4 Complete these sentences with *at* or *on*.

1.   The library is _____ Second Avenue.

2.   The library is _____ 413 Second Avenue.

3.   Mariko is _____ the library now.

4.   The post office is _____ the river.

5.   It's _____ 2020 River Street.

6.   Carlos is _____ the post office now.

7.   Carlos's apartment is also _____ River Street.

8.   My favorite coffee shop is _____ Main Street.

5 Form sentences with *in* or *on*.

Example: Miami / the U.S.A.
>   *Miami is in the U.S.A.*

1.   Paris / France
2.   Geneva / Switzerland
3.   Tokyo / Japan
4.   Chicago / Lake Michigan
5.   San Francisco / the Pacific Ocean
6.   Buenos Aires / Argentina
7.   Miami / the Atlantic Ocean
8.   Cairo / the Nile River

6 Are the sentences on page 27 true? Which are false? Use negatives to correct the false sentences. Then tell the true location of each place. Use an atlas or the Internet if necessary.

Examples: San Diego and San Francisco are in Oregon.

San Diego and San Francisco aren't in Oregon. They're in California.

1. Santa Barbara is in Oregon.
2. The Cascade Mountains are in Arizona.
3. Reno is on the Pacific Ocean.
4. Vancouver and Edmonton are in Washington.
5. Los Angeles is on the Pacific Ocean.
6. Seattle is on the Columbia River.
7. Phoenix and Tucson are in Nevada.
8. The Grand Canyon is in Arizona.

D. Using At and At the with Locations

At the and *at* are used with some locations. With other locations, *at the* and *at* are not used; only the place expression is used.

At the	At	No Preposition or Article
I am **at the bank.**	My sister is **at work.**	My brother is **there.**
at the beach	at church	downtown
at the hospital	at class	(over) here
at the library	at home*	(over) there
at the movies	at school	nearby
at the museum		
at the post office		
at the store		

*Note: People say both, "He's at home" and "He's home."

7 In a chain, ask and answer questions with *Where*. Use the following cues and add two of your own. Continue until each student has a turn. Use the chart on page 27 to help you.

Example: Ali / bank

George / school

A. Where's Ali?

B. He's at the bank. Where's George?

C. He's at school. Where's . . .

1. Anne / home
2. Carlos / downtown
3. Jack / museum
4. Fred / work
5. Jane / over there
6. Rick / post office

7. Lea / beach
8. Sandy / store
9. Mary / movies
10. Laura / church
11.   /
12.   /

8 Circle the correct words to complete this letter.

November 14
Dear Akiko,

Greetings from the United States! I am back ((in) / on) San Diego now. My apartment

(is / are) very small and expensive, but (it's / they're) nice. My roommate (is / are)
  1   2   3

friendly too! (She / Her) name is Anne, and she (is / are) from the United States.
                        4   5

(I / My) life here (is / are) very busy. I am (at / at the) school every day. My classes
      6   7   8

are (in / on) the afternoon and (in / at) night. In the morning, I am usually (at / at the)
              9   10   11

library. (There / They're) is always a lot of homework!
              12

(In / On) the weekends, I (am / are) busy too. San Diego (am / is) beautiful, and
   13   14   15

(it's / its) very interesting. There (is / are) a wonderful zoo here, and there (is / are) many
  16   17   18

parks. San Diego is (at / on) the Pacific Ocean, and there (is / are) thousands of boats
                   19   20

in the harbor. (I / My) am in love with the ocean!
         21

The weather (in / on) San Diego is usually very nice. (In / On) the morning, it's
               22   23

sometimes foggy. Most of the time, it's (sun / sunny) and dry.
                                      24

It's time to study again. I miss you a lot! I'm homesick today, but I really (am / is)
                                                                 25

happy here.

Love,
Mariko

Using What You've Learned

9   **Describing Places.**   Write sentences about your town or city. Try to write at least six sentences. Give both affirmative and negative sentences.

Example: *There are buses here.*
There isn't a subway here.

10   **Describing Locations.**   Where is your house or apartment?

■   Separate into pairs. In each pair, tell each other your street name and then give your specific address. Remember the information; do not write it.

■   Then, in your group, change partners. Give your first partner's street name and specific address to your new partner.

■   Your new partner must check the information with your first partner.

Example: A.   My apartment is on River Street. It's at 2020 River Street.
              B.   My house is on . . . It's at . . .
              B.   Carlos's apartment is on River Street. It's at 2020 River Street.
              C.   Ali's apartment . . .
              C.   Carlos, your apartment is on River Street. It's at 2020 River Street.
              A.   Correct!

11   **Writing Letters.**   Write a letter to someone who reads English. You can write to classmates in your class, or in another class. Use the letter in Activity 8 on pages 28 to 29 as an example. Tell about your life now—your studies, your apartment or home, and your city. "Mail" the letter in a box in your classroom, or e-mail the letters.

Video Activities: Venice

Before You Watch.

1. Where is the city of Venice? Circle the correct answer.

        a. France   b. Italy   c. Greece

2. Venice is famous because it has _____.

        a. old buildings   b. many canals   c. a lot of rain

Watch.   Check all the correct answers.

     Vocabulary Note: *To sink* means to go under the water. The past tense is *sank*.

1. What are Venice's problems?

   _____ The canals are crowded.

   _____ The water is very dirty.

   _____ There is a lot of air pollution.

   _____ No one wants to go there.

   _____ It is sinking.

2. Venice needs

   _____ money

   _____ tourists

   _____ water

Watch Again.

1. Complete the sentences with numbers from the box.

200	30	6,000,000	1

   1. Venice has about _____ canals.

   2. A few years ago Venice sank about _____ foot.

   3. They cleaned the canals _____ years ago.

   4. About _____ tourists visit Venice each year.

2. Bob Guthrie's group is called "_____ Venice."

        a. Visit   b. Stop   c. Save

After You Watch.   Use these nouns to write sentences about Venice with *there is* and *there are*.

Example: *There are a lot of boats in Venice.*

boats	water	money	canals
water pollution	old buildings	problems	tourists

1. _____

2. _____

3. _____

4. _____

5. _____

Chapter 2

Shopping and E-commerce

PART 1

The Present Continuous Tense: Affirmative Statements and Questions; *And; Too*

Setting the Context

Prereading Questions   Look at the picture below. What are the two friends looking for in the store?

Shopping for Gifts

Salesperson: Good morning. May I help you? Are you looking for something special?
Gloria: Yes, I'm looking for a birthday present for my friend.
Mike: I'm shopping for a birthday gift too.
Salesperson: Does she like perfume?
Gloria: Yes, but I'm thinking about clothing.
Mike: How about a sweater and a scarf?
Salesperson: Sweater and scarf sets are very popular this season. And we're having a sale on them right now.
Gloria: Great! Which color do you like?
Mike: Hmmm, I'm not sure. I'm deciding between the red and the blue.
Gloria: Well, pick one so we can go. We still need to bake the birthday cake!

Check Your Understanding

1.   Are Gloria and Mike buying something special?
2.   What kind of gift is Gloria thinking about?
3.   What is Mike's idea?
4.   What else are Gloria and Mike doing for their friend's birthday?

A. Affirmative Statements

Form	Subject + *be* + verb + *-ing*	
Long Form	**Contraction**	**Notes**
I am looking. You **are looking.** He She } **is looking.** It We You } **are looking.** They	**I'm looking.** You**'re looking.** He**'s** She**'s** } **looking.** It**'s** We**'re** You**'re** } **looking.** They**'re**	The present continuous tense tells about actions in progress now. Common time expressions with this tense are *now* or *right now*.

1 Underline all present continuous tense verbs in the conversation on page 32.

2 Use the present continuous to complete these sentences. Use the picture below and the verbs in parentheses for help.

1. Mike _____is buying_____ (buying) gifts.

2. The little boys _____ (playing).

3. The little girl and her mother _____ (taking) a walk.

4. They _____ (looking) at toys.

5. The teenage girls _____ (shopping) for new clothes.

6. The woman _____ (going) home.

7. The teenage boy _____ (listening) to music.

8. The old man _____ (reading) the newspaper.

B. Yes / No Questions and Short Answers

Form for Questions	*Be* + subject + verb + *ing*
Form for Short Answers	**Yes** + subject + verb **No** + subject + verb + **not**

Questions	Possible Answers	
	Affirmative	**Negative**
Are you **looking?**	Yes, I **am.**	No, **I'm not.**
Is he / she / it **looking?**	Yes, **he is.**	No, **he isn't.**
		No, **he's not.**
	Yes, **she is.**	No, **she isn't.**
		No, **she's not.**
	Yes, **it is.**	No, **it isn't.**
		No, **it's not.**
Are we **looking?**	Yes, **we are.**	No, **we aren't.**
		No, **we're not.**
Are you **looking?**	Yes, **we are.**	No, **we aren't.**
		No, **we're not.**
Are they **looking?**	Yes, **they are.**	No, **they aren't.**
		No, **they're not.**

3   Work with a partner. Take turns asking and answering these questions about the picture in Activity 2.

Example: A: Is the Mike buying gifts?
               B: Yes, he is.

1.   Is the woman carrying packages?

2.   Is the old man reading a book?

3.   Are the little boys playing?

4.   Are the boys riding bicycles?

5.   Is the teenage boy dancing?

6.   Is he carrying a radio?

7.   Is the little girl taking a walk with her father?

8.   Are we studying Chapter 2?

9.   Are you answering Question 9?

10.   Are you speaking Chinese now?

C. Information Questions with What

Form	What + be + subject + verb + -ing	
Statement		**Information Question**
She's buying a sweater. They are playing.		**What** is she buying? **What** are they doing?

4 What are these people doing? Ask and answer questions about the people.

Examples: A: *What is the little boy doing?*
              B: *He's playing.*

Playing!

1.

*trying on
a sweater*

2.

buying gifts

3.

writing a check

4.

resting

5.

BUS

waiting for the bus

6.

listening to music

7.

riding bicycles

8.

working on a computer

5 Ask and answer questions about the picture. Use the verbs below and make questions with *what*. Make at least six questions.

Example: A: *What are the little girls wearing?*

B: *They're wearing jackets and mittens.*

carrying	eating	riding
doing	reading	wearing
drinking		

D. And

	Examples	Notes
Two Sentences	I'm looking for new clothes. My friend is shopping for a gift.	*And* means "also" or "in addition." It can join two sentences. Use a comma before *and*.
One Sentence	I'm looking for new clothes, **and** my friend is shopping for a gift.	

6 Use *and* to join each pair of sentences. Remember to add a comma when you write each new sentence.

Example: I'm looking for new shoes.
My sister is buying a new purse.

I'm looking for new shoes, and my sister is buying a new purse.

1. Gloria is looking for some new clothes.
   The salesperson is helping her.
2. Cristina is buying a gift.
   Mario is looking for a birthday card.
3. Maria is having a birthday.
   Mike is shopping for a gift.
4. Mike is buying perfume.
   Cristina is buying a CD.
5. The old man is reading a newspaper.
   The teenage boy is listening to music.
6. We're going to a restaurant tonight.
   Our teacher is paying for the dinner.

7. I'm _____ after class.

   My friends are _____.

8. I'm _____ this weekend.

   My friends are _____.

E. Too *with Short Statements*

Long Form	Short Form	Notes
I'm spending a lot of money. My brother is spending a lot of money.	I'm spending a lot of money, **and** my brother **is too.**	Too means "also" in affirmative statements.
My brother is spending a lot of money. I'm spending a lot of money.	My brother is spending a lot of money, **and I am too.**	Do not use contractions in these statements.

7   Complete these sentences with a form of the verb *be* and the word *too*.

1. I'm looking for something special, and my friend __is__ __too.__

2. Cristina is going to the birthday party, and Mario _____ _____.

3. Mike is buying a gift, and I _____ _____.

4. I'm spending a lot of money, and you _____ _____.

5. Gloria is looking for a job, and I _____ _____.

6. Ann is working at the mall, and her friends _____ _____.

7. John is playing tennis this afternoon, and Miki _____ _____.

8. Jeff is watching television, and Jack _____ _____.

9. I'm studying English very hard, and my classmates _____ _____.

F. Descriptions—Questions with What + Noun

What + noun is used to ask for specific information. Many different nouns can be used in these questions. Compare the forms:

Question Word	Form	
What	**What + be +** subject + verb + **-ing**	
What kind (of)	**What kind (+ of +** noun**) + be +** subject + verb + **-ing**	
What + noun	**What +** noun **+ be +** subject + verb + **-ing**	
	Questions	**Possible Answers**
What	**What** are you looking for?	I'm looking for a sweater.
What kind (of)	**What kind of sweater** are you looking for?	I'm looking for a wool sweater.
	What kind are you looking for?	
	What color are you looking for?	I'm looking for a red sweater.
What + noun	**What size** are you looking for?	I'm looking for size medium.

8   Read this dialogue. Then use the vocabulary below to create three different dialogues. Choose one dialogue and role play it. Ask your teacher for help with new vocabulary.

Example:

Salesperson: May I help you?
Gloria: I'm looking for <u>a birthday present.</u>
         I'm buying <u>a gift</u> for <u>my friend.</u>
Salesperson: What <u>kind of gift</u> are you looking for?
Gloria: <u>Clothes or perfume.</u>
Salesperson: How about this?

VOCABULARY

			color	size
casual	clothes	a birthday	light blue	
elegant	a coat	an interview	dark blue	
inexpensive	a gift	a party	red	
nice	shoes	school	white, etc.	
serious	a suit	a trip		small
special	a sweater	a wedding		medium
warm		work		large
stylish		a date		size 12, size 36, etc.

1.
A.   May I help you?
B.   I'm looking for _____.
      I'm buying _____ for _____.
A.   What _____ are you looking for?
B.   _____.
A.   How about this?

2.
A.   May I help you?
B.   I'm looking for _____.
      I'm buying _____ for _____.
A.   What _____ are you looking for?
B.   _____.
A.   How about this?

3.
A.   May I help you?
B.   I'm looking for _____.
      I'm buying _____ for _____.

A. What _____ _____ are you looking for?

B. _____.

A. How about this?

> In stores, sales people ask "May I help you?" or "Are you looking for something special?" If you aren't, you can say, "No, thank you. I'm just looking" or "Just looking, thank you."

Using What You've Learned

9   **Telling Stories.**   Look at the picture in Activity 2 on page 33. Tell a story about one or more of the people. For example, who is the woman in the picture? What is she carrying? Where is she going? What is she thinking about?

10   **Describing People.**   Write your name on a piece of paper. Your teacher will collect all the names and put them in a bag. Then choose a name, but do not say it. What is that person wearing? Describe the person's clothing, but do not tell the person's name. Other students guess the name.

Example: A: This student is wearing a white sweater, blue jeans, leather boots, and one gold earring.

B: It's Anna!

C: No, it isn't. It's Antonio.

11   **Creating Stories.**   This is a picture of a birthday party. Create a story about it. Who is at the party? What is everyone doing?

PART 2

Spelling Rules; Negative Statements; Using *But*

Setting the Context

Ordering from a Catalogue

Prereading Questions   In this picture, two friends are talking about shopping. What are they thinking about?

Michelle: Hi, Donna. What are you doing?
Donna: I'm ordering from this new catalogue.
Michelle: What are you buying?
Donna: I'm not sure. I'm thinking about this bathing suit and some new jeans.
Michelle: I'm going to the mall right now. Do you want to come with me?
Donna: No, thanks. I'm trying not to spend any money today.
Michelle: But aren't you shopping right now?
Donna: Yes, but only from a catalogue. The bill won't come for two weeks, so I'm not actually spending any money now!

Check Your Understanding

1. What is Donna doing?
2. Where is Michelle going?
3. Is Donna going with her?
4. Do you like to shop from catalogues? Why or why not?

A. Spelling Rules with -ing

Ending	-ing Spelling
Consonant and -e drive use make write	Drop the -e and add -ing. driving using making writing
One vowel and one consonant (one-syllable words) get sit shop run	Double the final consonant and add -ing. getting sitting shopping running
Other endings buy snow fix study look try pay work rest	Add -ing. buying snowing fixing studying looking trying paying working resting

1   Underline all present continuous verbs in the conversation on page 40.

2   Write the -ing forms of these verbs.

1. sit _____*sitting*_____
2. shop _____
3. study _____
4. buy _____
5. rest _____
6. make _____
7. use _____
8. run _____
9. pay _____
10. take _____
11. eat _____
12. sleep _____
13. get _____
14. drive _____

3   Use the present continuous tense to complete these sentences.

1. Donna _____ (buy) a gift.
2. She _____ (write) a check. She _____ (use) a pen.
3. Peter _____ (make) a list.
4. She _____ (draw) a picture, and he _____ (cut) some paper.
5. He _____ (sleep).
6. She _____ (study).
7. He _____ (look) out the window.
8. She _____ (ride) a bicycle. Her dog _____ (run) after the bicycle.
9. She _____ (sit) on the sofa. She _____ (watch) TV.

B. Negative Statements

Form	Subject + *be* + *not* + verb + *-ing*	
Long Form	**Contraction**	
I am not working. You **are not working.** He ⎫ She ⎬ **is not working.** It ⎭ We ⎫ You ⎬ **are not working.** They ⎭	**I'm not working.** You're **not working.** He's ⎫ She's ⎬ **not working.** It's ⎭ We're ⎫ You're ⎬ **not working.** They're ⎭	You **aren't working.** He ⎫ She ⎬ **isn't working.** It ⎭ We ⎫ You ⎬ **aren't working.** They ⎭

4   These sentences have negative contractions. Give the other form of each negative contraction.

Example: *We're not spending money.*
           We aren't spending money.

1.   She's not buying new clothes.
2.   He's not using a credit card.
3.   They're not spending money.
4.   We're not eating in restaurants.
5.   It's not working right now.
6.   You're not driving the car now.
7.   We're not shopping from catalogues.
8.   They're not looking at stores on the Internet.

Many people around the world shop at shopping malls, but now many people shop from home, too. They buy from catalogues, or shop on the Internet. Do you shop online?

5   Make negative sentences from these cues. Use the contraction *they're*. Use *now* or *right now.*

Example: *not look for a present right now*
           They're not looking for a present right now.

1.   not eat in restaurants
2.   not shop online
3.   not buy new clothes
4.   not use the Internet
5.   not go to the mall
6.   not use credit cards

C. But

	Examples	Notes
Two Sentences	I am buying a tie. My friend is just looking.	*But* shows a difference or contrast. It can join two sentences. Use a comma before *but*.
One Sentence	I am buying a tie, **but** my friend is just looking.	

6   Use *but* to join each pair of sentences. Remember to add a comma when you write each new sentence.

Example: *Our friends are spending a lot of money now.*
We're trying to save.
Our friends are spending a lot of money now, but we're trying to save.

1. My co-workers are going out to lunch.
   I'm eating a sandwich at my desk.

2. Our friends are going to the movies now.
   Donna and I are staying home.

3. Joe is spending a lot right now.
   Donna is saving her money.

4. Jane is buying a new bathing suit right now.
   Donna is wearing her old one.

5. Mary is using her credit card.
   Donna is paying in cash.

6. Robert is shopping on line.
   Peter is shopping from catalogues.

Using What You've Learned

7   **Pantomiming.**   In a small group, write the *-ing* form of these verbs on pieces of paper. You may add other verbs to the list.

buy	listen	shop
carry	look	study
dance	pay	take
decide	play	think
help	read	work

Fold the pieces of paper. Each student picks one and acts out the verb. Do not use words, just actions. The other students guess what the student is doing. Take turns acting out all the verbs.

Example: shopping (*written on a piece of paper*)

> A: (*acts out shopping*)
> B: Are you carrying something?
> A: No, I'm not.
> C: Are you shopping?
> A: Yes, I am.

8 Food Shopping.   You are in the grocery store, buying food for a class party. Each person tells what they are shopping for, looking for, or buying.

Example: A: I'm shopping for juice.
B: I'm looking for the candy.
C: I'm buying potato chips.

Make a list of all the food items. Go shopping and have a real party!

PART 3   # More Prepositions of Place; *There is / There are* + subject + verb + *-ing*; *It* Versus *There*

Setting the Context

Prereading Questions   In this picture, a TV station is filming a program. Who is in the picture, and where are these people?

Live from the Mall

Broadcaster: "It's a busy afternoon, and right now we're broadcasting live from the mall. There are a lot of people shopping today! Right now, I'm standing in front of Discount Drugs. It's next to Max-Mart and across from Famous Fashions."

"Here's a shopper! Excuse me, sir. What are you buying today?"
Shopper: "I'm buying skis for cross-country skiing."

Check Your Understanding Circle T for *True* or F for *False.*

1. T F The mall is busy today.
2. T F A television crew is broadcasting at the mall.
3. T F The announcer is standing in front of Max-Mart.
4. T F The man is buying water skis.

A. More Prepositions of Place

to the left / right of	next to	across from
over / under	between	in front of / in back of
near / far from	on top of	

1 Look at this map of the mall. Imagine you are standing at the main entrance. Circle T for *True* or F for *False* for each sentence about the map. Correct the false sentences.

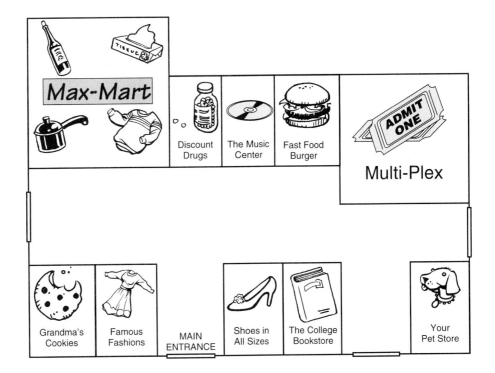

1. T F Discount Drugs is next to ~~Fast Food Burgers.~~ *Max-Mart.*
2. T F Discount Drugs is across from Famous Fashions.
3. T F Discount Drugs is near Grandma's Cookies.
4. T F Grandma's Cookies is far from the Multi-Plex Cinema.
5. T F The College Bookstore is between Shoes in All Sizes and Fast Food Burger.

6. T F Your Pet Store is to the left of Max-Mart.
7. T F The Music Center is between Grandma's Cookies and Famous Fashions.
8. T F The Music Center is to the right of Famous Fashions.
9. T F Discount Drugs is under the Multi-Plex Cinema.

2 Use the same map to help you. Complete these sentences with a preposition of place.

1. There is a drugstore _____ Max-Mart.

2. There is a music store _____ Grandma's Cookies and Famous Fashions.

3. There is a cinema _____ Grandma's Cookies.

4. There is a drug store _____ the cinema.

5. There is a music store _____ a fast food restaurant.

6. There is a shoe store _____ The College Bookstore.

7. There is a pet store _____ Discount Drugs.

B. There is/There are + *subject* + *verb* + -ing

Form	Subject + *be* + verb + *-ing*	*There* + *be* + subject + verb + *-ing*
	Without *there*	**With *there***
	A lot of people **are shopping.**	**There are** a lot of people **shopping.**
	A girl **is looking** for shoes.	**There is** a girl **looking** for shoes.
	A boy **is buying** some toys.	**There is** a boy **buying** some toys.

3 Use these verbs to complete the sentences on page 47. Then add two original sentences.

carrying	playing	sitting
✓ listening	reading	talking

1.   There are some teenage girls _listening_ to music.

2.   There is a young man _____ presents.

3.   There are two young women _____.

4.   There is a woman _____ on a bench.

5.   There is an old man _____ the newspaper.

6.   There are two little boys _____.

7.   _____

8.   _____

4   Use these cues to make sentences with *there is* or *there are* + verb + *-ing*.

Examples: a parrot / say hello
        There is a parrot saying hello.
        two birds / sing
        There are two birds singing.

1.   a dog / bark
2.   three cats / meow
3.   a monkey / climb a ladder
4.   a fish / swim in the water
5.   a mouse / sit in a cage
6.   two rabbits / eat lettuce

C. It *Versus* There

	Examples	Notes
It	**It's** 12:30 P.M. **It's** July 4th. **It's** summer. **It's** hot.	*It* is used with time and weather expressions.
There	**There are** people at the beach. **There is** a park nearby. **There are** children playing.	*There* is used to show that something exists or is in a place.

5   Use *it* or *there* to complete these sentences about a mall in Canada.

1. _____*It*_____'s January, and _____*it*_____'s cold and snowy. _____ are a lot of people buying snow shovels.

2. _____ are a lot of people buying flowers and candy. Why? Because _____ is February, and _____ is Valentine's Day.

3. _____ are a lot of people getting tickets to Florida. Why? Because _____'s March, and _____'s still cold and snowy in the north.

4. _____'s April. _____'s raining. _____ are a lot of people carrying umbrellas.

5. _____ is May. _____ is Mother's Day. _____ are a lot of people buying roses.

6. _____ are a lot of people shopping for wedding presents. Why? Because _____'s June, and _____'s the month for weddings.

7. _____ are a lot of people looking for bathing suits. Why? Because _____'s July, and _____'s hot.

8. _____ are a lot of people buying school clothes. Why? Because _____ is August, and _____'s back-to-school time.

9. _____'s September. _____'s autumn. _____ are a lot of people buying rakes for raking leaves.

10. _____ are a lot of people buying costumes. Why? Because _____ is October, and _____ is Halloween.

11. _____'s November. _____'s windy outside. _____ are a lot of people wearing coats and gloves.

12. _____ is December. _____ is the holiday season. _____ are a lot of people shopping for presents.

Using What You've Learned

6   **Describing Locations.**   Look around your class. Who is sitting in front of you? Who is sitting next to you? Are you sitting near the door? Write two statements about your location in the classroom, but do not put your name on your paper. Your teacher will collect the papers and read them. Guess who each person is.

Example: *Teacher:* I'm sitting across from Miguel. I'm sitting in front of Akiko.
             Student: It's Mei!

7   **Describing Places.**   What is your favorite place? What is your favorite time of the year there? Is your favorite place a beach in December? Or is it a city in the spring? Bring a picture of your favorite place to class or draw a picture of it. Imagine you are not in class, and you are at your favorite place. Describe the season and the weather, and tell about the people and things around you.

Example: It's September in Chile. It's warm. I'm playing my guitar on the beach.
            There are a lot of people enjoying the beautiful weather.

8   **Role-Playing.**   Role-play the following situations.

1.   You and your friend are at the bookstore. You are looking for school supplies. Ask for help.
2.   You and your friend are at a music store. You are looking for your favorite CDs. You also want to buy a CD for your parents. Ask for help.

PART 4

To and *To the* with Locations; *Because*

Setting the Context

Prereading Questions   In this picture, a TV news team is filming a program. Where are they filming? What are the other people in the picture doing?

Lottery Jackpot

A: "We're standing here in front of the Mini-Mart. A lot of people behind me are buying lottery tickets because there is a $20,000,000 jackpot. Excuse me, sir. Are you buying a lottery ticket?"
B: "Yes, I'm buying several tickets."
A: "What will you do if you win?"
B: "If? You mean *when*. I already have a plan:

- Go to the bank to deposit half the money.
- Go to work to quit my job.
- Go to the hospital to donate some money.
- Go to the store to buy a bathing suit and shorts.
- Go to the beach to relax and think about where to go next."

Check Your Understanding

1. What are these people doing at the Mini-Mart?
2. Does this man think he will win? Does he have a plan?
3. Do you buy lottery tickets? Why or why not?

A. To *and* To the *with Locations*

To or *to the* is used with some locations. With other locations, *to* or *to the* is *not* used; only the place expression is used.

To	To the	No Preposition or Article
I'm going **to church.**	I'm going **to the bank.**	I'm going **downtown.**
to church	to the bank	downtown
to class	to the beach	home
to school	to the hospital	(over) there
to work	to the library	
	to the movies	
	to the museum	
	to the post office	
	to the store	

1   Look at the reading on page 50. Underline all the uses of *go to* and circle the locations.

2   Make sentences with the cues below and *She's going* or *She's going to*.

Example: store

She's going to the store.

1. bank   5. school   8. museum
2. post office   6. work   9. downtown
3. home   7. movies   10. beach
4. there

B. Because

	Examples	Notes
Two Sentences	I'm buying a **soccer ball.** I like **to play soccer.**	**Because** shows the reason for something. It joins two sentences.
One Sentence	I'm buying a soccer ball **because** I like to play soccer.	

3   You are shopping. Your partner is a salesperson. Explain what you are looking for. Make three sentences with *because*. Then change roles.

Example: a heavy jacket / not like the cold

I'm looking for a heavy jacket because I don't like the cold.

1. a suitcase / like to travel
2. a nice suit / have an interview
3. a French dictionary / need to learn French
4. yarn / want to knit a sweater
5. skis / love to ski
6. computer / like to surf the Internet

4 Complete this story with the present continuous tense. Use the verbs in parentheses. Use negative forms when you see *not*.

Jack's wife, Julie, is very happy. She _is smiling_ (smile) a lot today. Why? Because Jack is the lottery winner! Right now Julie _____ (not work). She _____ (sit) at home with her friends. She _____ (talk) about her travel plans. Her friends _____ (not listen) because they _____ (dream) about the lottery. Right now Jack _____ (shop) for things for the trip. But Jack _____ (not feel) happy. He _____ (feel) tired, and he _____ (dream) about his old life.

Using What You've Learned

5 **At the Mall.**   You see your classmates at the mall. Ask each other questions about what you are doing. Use *because* in your answers.

Example: A.   Hi, Louis. What are you shopping for?
             B.   Hi, Annie. I'm looking for a new television because my old TV doesn't work. What are you doing, Alex?
             C: I'm going to the cinema because there's a new movie I want to see.

Checking Your Progress

Check your progress with structures from Chapters 1 and 2. Be sure to review any problem areas.

Part 1.   Choose the correct word(s) to complete each sentence.

1. Mariela _____ from Colombia.
   a. am
   b. is
   c. are
   d. goes
   e. going

2. _____ is George? He's 25.
   a. When
   b. Why
   c. How old
   d. How
   e. Where

3. John is doing _____ homework.
   a. her
   b. he
   c. she
   d. we
   e. his

4. Sandy is tired, _____ I'm not.
   a. and
   b. but
   c. because
   d. or
   e. so

5. Jim is going_____
  a. at the downtown.
  b. to the downtown.
  c. downtown.
  d. to downtown.
  e. for downtown.

6. Why _____ there?
  a. she going
  b. she goes
  c. is she going
  d. is going she
  e. she is going

7. _____ cold outside.
  a. It's
  b. There
  c. Is
  d. There's
  e. Its

8. Al was born _____ March 18.
  a. in
  b. on
  c. at
  d. from
  e. to

9. _____ is Paul studying now? At the library.
  a. When
  b. Where
  c. Why
  d. How
  e. What

10. Paul's house is _____ 4218 Yuma Drive.
  a. in
  b. on
  c. to
  d. from
  e. at

Part 2. Circle the correct words to complete this story. Circle "X" to show that nothing is necessary.

(Its / It's) almost summer vacation. We (is / are) saving money now because we are
        1   2

(planning / planing) a trip. On our vacation, we are going (to / to the) beach. We are
        3   4

leaving (on / in) Friday. We are going (X / to) stay at a hotel (across from / on top of) the
        5   6   7

beach. Near the hotel, (it / there) is a park and a small shopping mall. It's (a / an) beau-
                              8   9

tiful place. My husband is excited about the trip, (and / but) I am too!
                                                              10

Video Activities: Online Pharmacies

Before You Watch.

1. Which of these stores sell medicine?
    - a. a pharmacy
    - b. a bakery
    - c. a hardware store

2. What is a prescription?
    - a. a kind of medicine
    - b. doctor's permission to buy a type of medicine

Watch.

1. What is the message of this video?
    - a. Don't buy drugs online.
    - b. Be careful when you buy drugs online.
    - c. Always buy drugs online.

2. What is happening to drug sales on the Internet?
    - a. More and more people are buying drugs online.
    - b. Not many people are buying drugs online.
    - c. Online pharmacies are not popular.

Watch Again.

1. Complete the following chart.

Sale of Drugs Online

Year	Amount
2000	_____
2001	$400,000,000
_____	$1,100,000,000
2003	_____
_____	_____

2. Check the benefits of buying drugs online

    _____ accountability   _____ convenience
    _____ price   _____ privacy
    _____ reliability   _____ safety

After You Watch.   Combine the following sentences with *and . . . too* or *but*.

1. I'm buying books online. My friend is buying books online.
2. Many people are buying lifestyle drugs online. They aren't buying antibiotics.
3. An antibiotic kills germs. A lifestyle drug doesn't kill germs.
4. You need a prescription to buy antibiotics. You need a prescription to buy lifestyle drugs.
5. Online bookstores are popular. Online pharmacies are popular.

Chapter 3

Friends and Family

PART 1

The Simple Present Tense: Affirmative Statements; Spelling and Pronunciation

Setting the Context

Prereading Questions   Look at the three pictures. What are the people doing?

The Modern Family

In today's modern world, there are many different kinds of families. There are large families, like the Sommas. They have eight children. Loretta and Steve Mason have a small family. They have two children. Some children live in single-parent homes, like Ricky Jones. He lives with his mother, Rita. In today's families, parents and children help around the house. Everyone does different chores like vacuuming, washing clothes, and taking out the garbage.   5

Check Your Understanding   Circle T for *True* or F for *False.*

1. T F Mr. and Mrs. Somma have a small family.
2. T F Loretta and Steve Mason have eight children.
3. T F Rita Jones has one child.
4. T F Ricky Jones lives in a single-parent home.
5. T F In today's families, only parents work around the house.

A. The Verb Have—Affirmative Statements

Form	Subject + *have*	Subject + *has*
I You We They	**have** a house.	He She It **has** a house.

1 Use *have* or *has* to complete these sentences.

1. I'm Rose Somma. There are ten people in my family! I __*have*__ a mother, a father, and seven sisters and brothers. I also _____ many cousins. My oldest cousin is married. She _____ a daughter and a baby boy. My other cousins aren't married.

2. I'm Steve Mason. Loretta and I _____ a small family. I come from a bigger family. I _____ three sisters and two brothers. All of us are married. We all _____ children, too. So my mother _____ 11 grandchildren.

3. I'm Ricky Jones. We _____ a very small family. I _____ only a mother. But my mother _____ five brothers and sisters, so we _____ a lot of relatives.

B. The Verb Do—Affirmative Statements

Form	Subject + *do*	Subject + *does*
I You We They	**do** a lot of work.	He She It **does** a lot of work.
Expressions		
do dishes **do** errands **do** homework **do** housework **do** laundry		***do*** + verb + ***-ing*** **do** cleaning **do** gardening **do** (grocery) shopping

2 Use *do* or *does* to complete this reading.

   We have a lot of housework in the Somma family. We all __*do*__ chores in our house. My mother _____ the grocery shopping. She also _____ the laundry, but my older sisters _____ the ironing. My younger sisters _____ the vacuuming. I _____ the dishes every morning, and my brother _____ the dishes every night. My father _____ most of the cooking. He also _____ the gardening. We all _____ housework every day. We try hard to keep our house clean!

In some U.S. households, the entire family helps with housework. Even young children have household chores. Sometimes children get money for doing chores. This money is called an *allowance*. Women still do most of the housework, but today husbands help much more than in the past. Who does the chores in your family?

C. Simple Present Tense of Other Verbs— Affirmative Statements

Form	Subject + verb	Subject + verb + -s	Notes
I You We They	**work** a lot.	He She **works** a lot. It	The simple present tense is used to talk about facts, opinions, and habits or schedules. Time expressions with this tense include *every day, every week, always,* and *sometimes.*

3   Use the verb at the beginning of each paragraph to complete the reading.

work (s)

Joe Somma is 19 years old. He _works_ at a grocery store. He _____ 40 hours a week. His younger brothers _____ at a car wash. They _____ part-time, ten hours a week. Joe's father _____ at a gas station, and his mother _____ at a department store. They all _____ very hard.

love (s)

Grandpa Somma is 80 years old. He _loves_ his family. Every afternoon he _____ to visit his grandchildren. They _____ Grandpa Somma. He _____ to tell stories. They _____ to hear the stories.

eat (s)

Pepper is the Sommas' dog. She likes food. She _eats_ a lot. Every morning, the children _____ breakfast in the kitchen. The dog _____ breakfast outside. After school, the boys _____ a snack. Pepper _____ with them.

In the U.S., many young people have jobs while they are going to school. Many high school students work after school, on weekends, and during the summer. University students frequently have jobs to help pay for their education.

D. Pronunciation

/s/ after /f/, /k/, /p/, and /t/		/z/ after /b/, /d/, /l/, /m/, /n/, /r/, /v/, and Vowel Sounds		
laughs*	sleeps	robs	comes	loves
works	hates	needs	listens	plays
		calls	tours	sees

*In this case, the pronunciation of *gh* is /f/.

4   Look at the list of verbs above. Repeat the words after your teacher. Underline the letters for each sound before the letter *s*.

Examples: lau<u>gh</u>s

   wor<u>k</u>s

5   Use these cues to make sentences about Rose. Take turns reading the sentences aloud. Pay attention to the pronunciation of the *-s* ending.

Example: get up very early
   Rose gets up very early.

1.   eat breakfast

2.   drink a cup of tea

3.   walk to school

4.   work hard at school

5.   think a lot about the future

6.   want a job at a newspaper

6   Use these cues to make sentences about Mrs. Somma. Take turns reading the sentences aloud. Pay attention to the pronunciation of the *-s* ending.

Example: listen to the radio every morning.
   Mrs. Somma listens to the radio every morning.

1.   prepare breakfast

2.   drive to the train station

3.   arrive at work at 10:00 A.M.

4.   come home at 6:00 P.M.

5.   clean the house at night

6.   stay up late

E. Spelling and Pronunciation (1)

Words Ending in Consonant + *y*		Words Ending in Vowel + *y*		Notes
cry	cries	buy	buys	Verbs with *y* endings sometimes change spelling. These verbs have the /z/ pronunciation. Verbs that have a vowel before the *y* do not change from *y* to *i*.
study	studies	enjoy	enjoys	
try	tries	play	plays	
		say	says	

7 Use the verbs in parentheses to complete the readings about the Somma family. Pay attention to spelling.

1. My brother Mike _tries_ (try) hard in school. He _____ (study) a lot. He also _____ (spend) a lot of time on sports. He _____ (play) a lot of different sports. He especially _____ (enjoy) swimming and soccer. He _____ (hate) to be bored.

2. My father _____ (work) very hard. In fact, he usually _____ (stay) at the gas station until late at night. He _____ (say) that he _____ (try) to take a vacation. But he never _____ (have) time. He _____ (worry) a lot about money. I worry a lot about him. Money _____ (buy) food, but money doesn't _____ (buy) good health.

F. Spelling and Pronunciation (2)

Words Ending in *ch, sh, ss, x,* and *z*				Notes
watch	watch**es**	fix	fix**es**	Add *-es* to words ending in *ch, sh, ss, x,* and *z*. The pronunciation is /ez/ or /iz/.
wash	wash**es**	buzz	buzz**es**	
kiss	kiss**es**			

Words Ending in *o*				Notes
do	do**es**	potato	potato**es**	Words ending in *o* sometimes add *-es*. The pronunciation is /z/.
go	go**es**	tomato	tomato**es**	

8 Complete these readings with the simple present forms of the verbs in parentheses. Pay attention to spelling.

1. My mother _does_ (do) many things for me. Early in the morning, she _____ (push) me out of bed. She _____ (fix) breakfast and then _____ (wash) the dishes. She _____ (kiss) me good-bye and _____

(watch) me walk down the block to school. Then she quickly _____ (do) some housework before she _____ (go) to work. My mom never _____ (relax).

    2. Ricky Jones __enjoys__ (enjoy) family picnics. His mother _____ (have) a large family, and they _____ (get) together for picnics in the summer. Rita Jones _____ (fix) salad and dessert, and her brothers and sisters _____ (buy) food for a barbecue. Grandma always _____ (make) cookies.

    Ricky _____ (play) ball with his older cousins. He _____ (try) hard to hit the ball, and sometimes he _____ (do). He _____ (watch) his cousins hit home runs all the time. He _____ (enjoy) the games, but his grandma _____ (kiss) him too much!

Using What You've Learned

9 **Telling About Families.**   Do you have a small family or a large family?

- For homework, find a picture of your family to bring to class.
- For homework, write a paragraph about your family. Use the ideas in Activity 1 on page 57 to help you.
- In class, work with a partner. Read your paragraph to your partner. Your partner is going to write down your paragraph.
- Listen to your partner's paragraph and write it down.
- Attach your picture to your paragraph. Look at all the pictures and read all the paragraphs.

10   **Talking About Housework.**   What are the chores in a typical house? Who does the chores?

■ Take turns telling about the Sommas and their chores. (See Activity 2 on page 57.)

■ Then fill in the chart about your family. Write in the names of your family members on the chart. Put checks in the boxes.

■ Tell the students in your group who does the chores in your home.

The Somma Family					
	Rose	**Mother**	**Father**	**Sisters**	**Brothers**
the cleaning	✓	✓	✓	✓	✓
the cooking			✓		
the dishes	✓				✓
the grocery shopping		✓			
the laundry		✓		✓	
the gardening			✓		
My Family					
the cleaning					
the cooking					
the dishes					
the grocery shopping					
the laundry					
the gardening					

11   **Telling Stories.**   Do you like to write stories?

■ Read the paragraph in Activity 3 on page 58 again about Joe's work.

■ Write a different paragraph about Joe and his family. Give Joe and his family new lives. Change their jobs and schedules.

■ Read your new paragraph to the class.

12   **Talking About Relatives.**   Do you have a favorite relative?

■ Bring a picture of one person in your family. Write a short paragraph about your relative. Don't write his or her name.

■ Your teacher will collect your paragraphs and pictures and put them around the room.

■ Look at the pictures and read the other students' paragraphs. Can you find the relative of each person in the class?

PART 2	# Adverbs of Frequency; Questions and Short Answers; Negative Statements

Setting the Context

Prereading Questions   Who lives here? Is his room neat?

Life Is Tough

Mothers! Sometimes they can drive you crazy! How often does your mom tell you to clean up your room? My mother always tells me to pick up my clothes, put away my books, make my bed, etc., etc., etc. I usually try to make my   5 room neat, but sometimes I forget. Then she gets upset. Sure, it's true. My mom doesn't have time to do everything. But I don't either. She never understands me.

Check Your Understanding   Circle T for *True* or F for *False*.

1. T F Ricky's mother always drives him crazy.
2. T F His mother never tells him to clean up his room.
3. T F He always remembers to make his room neat.
4. T F His mother has a lot of time.

A. Adverbs of Frequency—Always, Usually, Often, Sometimes, Seldom, Rarely, Never

	Form	Subject + adverb + verb	
100%	**always**	I	
90%	**usually/generally**	You	
75%	**often**	We	**always** get up early.
50%	**sometimes**	They	
10%	**seldom/rarely**	Bill	
0%	**never**	Sam	**never** gets up early.
		Mary	

1   Work with a partner. Talk about your *own* habits and activities. Use the following cues. Use one of these adverbs in each sentence: *always, usually, often, sometimes, seldom, never.*

Example: go to bed late

    I sometimes go to bed late.
  or *I always go to bed late.*
  or *I never go to bed late.*

1. get up early
2. eat a big breakfast
3. take the bus to school
4. drive to school
5. get to class on time
6. have lunch
7. read the local newspaper
8. cook dinner
9. do my homework
10. study English grammar very carefully

B. Adverbs of Frequency with the Verb Be

Form		Subject + *be* + adverb of frequency		Notes
I	am	**always**	hungry.	With the verb *be*, the adverbs of frequency come after the subject + verb.
She	is	**often**	late.	
We	are	**usually**	tired.	
They	are	**never**	early.	

2 Talk about your roommate, friend, husband, wife, or parents. Use an adverb of frequency in each sentence. Use the cues below.

Example: be late

My husband is always late.

1. be kind
2. be happy
3. be on time
4. be nervous
5. be bored

6. be hungry
7. be lonely
8. be busy
9. be tired

C. Questions with Who

Questions	Short answers with *do* or *does*		Notes
	Affirmative	**Negative**	
Who + verb + *-s* (+ object)	I	I	*Do, does, don't,* and *doesn't* are auxiliary or helping verbs. Use them for short answers, negative statements, and questions for all present tense verbs except the verb *be*. Questions with *who* are usually singular.
Who cleans the house?	You	You	
Who washes the dishes?	We } **do.**	We } **don't.**	
	They	They	
	He	He	
	She } **does.**	She } **doesn't.**	
	It	It	

3 Look back at your chore chart from Activity 10 on page 64. Use those cues to ask and answer questions. Make questions with *who*. Give short answers with *do* or *does*. Then add questions from the pie chart below.

Example: usually make breakfast

      A.   In your family, who usually makes breakfast?

      B.   My mother usually does.

    or   My father often does.

    or   I do. My wife never does.

D. Negative Statements

Long Form			
Form	**Subject + *do not* + verb**		**Subject + *does not* + verb**
I You We They	**do not wash** dishes.		He She It **does not wash** dishes.
Contractions			
Form	**Subject + *don't* + verb**		**Subject + *doesn't* + verb**
I You We They	**don't cook.**		He She It **doesn't cook.**

Note: Don't and *doesn't* are auxiliary or helping verbs. Use them to make present tense verbs negative, except the verb *be*.

4 Use *don't* or *doesn't* to complete these sentences. Then write *true* or *false* after each statement.

1.   Most people _____*don't*_____ like to do chores. _____*true*_____

2.   My family _____ travel often. _____

3. We _____ have pets at home. _____

4. My friends _____ like to go to the movies. _____

5. Ricky Jones _____ have brothers or sisters. _____

6. My best friend _____ study English. _____

7. I _____ have a lot of time to do chores. _____

8. Our teacher _____ give us enough homework. _____

5 Write five things you never do. Write five things your friend, roommate, husband, wife, or parent never does. Then work in groups and share your information.

Example: *I don't smoke. I don't drive fast.*
My roommate doesn't go to bed early. She doesn't speak my language.

ME

MY _____

1. _____   _____

2. _____   _____

3. _____   _____

4. _____   _____

5. _____   _____

E. Yes / No Questions

Form	*Do* + subject + verb	*Does* + subject + verb
Do { I, you, we, they }	**clean** everyday?	**Does** { he, she, it } **help** very often?

6 Ask and answer the following questions. Listen when your partner asks a question. Don't read the question. Look only at each other.

STUDENT A

1. Do you have a small family or a large family?
2. Do all of the people in your family live in this city?
3. Do you often call or e-mail your friends?
4. Do your relatives speak English?
5. Now ask two more questions with *do* or *does*.

STUDENT B

1. Does your family take vacation together?
2. Does your father cook?
3. Do your brothers or sisters speak English?
4. Do your friends often call you?
5. Now ask two more questions with *do* or *does*.

F. Information Questions with How often

Statement	I study every night.
	She studies every night.
Yes/No Question	*Do* or *does* + subject + verb
	Do you study every night?
	Does she study every night?
Information Question	Question word + *do* or *does* + subject + verb
	How often do you study?
	How often does she study?

 **7**   Ask and answer questions about the people below. Make questions with *how often*.

Example: A.   How often does she study?
          B.   She studies every night.

1.

2.

3.

4.

5.

6.

Using What You've Learned

8   **Asking Questions.**

■   Write eight interesting questions for a classmate using *how often*.

■   Take turns asking and answering each other's questions.

1.   How often *do you use a computer?*

2.   How often _____

3.   How often _____

4.   How often _____

5.   How often _____

6.   How often _____

7.   How often _____

8.   How often _____

9   **Asking Questions.**   A questionnaire is a list of questions.

■   Write a questionnaire with eight questions about family life.

■   Ask three students to answer the questions.

■   Finally, share the answers with the class.

Example: *Do you work?*
Who cooks in your house?
How often do you shop for groceries?
Does your husband/wife wash the clothes?

PART 3   # Commands: Common Verbs + Infinitives

Setting the Context

Prereading Questions   Where does this boy do his homework? Where do you do your homework?

Parents and Children

Loretta: Michael, you have to move your books. We need to set the table for dinner.

Michael: I don't want to set the table now. I'm still doing my homework.

Loretta: But you need to help around the house sometimes! You know that.

Michael: I know, but I have to finish my math homework first.

Loretta: OK. Turn off the TV, and let's do the homework together. Then after we finish, let's set the table. OK?

Check Your Understanding   Circle T for *True* or F for *False*.

1.   T F It's time for lunch at this house.
2.   T F Michael needs to set the table.
3.   T F Michael has spelling homework.
4.   T F Loretta wants to do the homework with Michael.

A. Commands

Affirmative	Negative	Notes
Sit down, please.	**Don't stand** up.	Use this form for *you*. For politeness, add *please*.
Let's go out.	**Let's not stay** in.	Use this form for *we*.

Note: Let's is a contraction of *Let us.*

1   Underline all commands in the opening conversation on page 68.

2   Loretta is talking to Michael. Use these verbs to make commands. Use *don't* for negative commands.

    be   comb   fight   take   watch
    clean   do   make   wash

1.   *Take* _____ out the garbage.

2.   *Don't make* _____ a mess! (negative)

3.   _____ your room!

4.   _____ your face!

5.   _____ your hair!

6.   _____ your homework!

7.   _____ with your brother! (negative)

8.   _____ late! (negative)

9.   _____ TV until you finish your homework! (negative)

10. _____ the dishes!

3   Now Loretta and Michael will work together. Change Loretta's commands from the *you* form to the *we* form.

Example: *Wash the dishes!*
            Let's wash the dishes.

1.   Clean your room!
2.   Make your bed!
3.   Take out the garbage!
4.   Do the laundry!
5.   Turn off the TV!
6.   Eat dinner!
7.   Read your assignment!
8.   Practice your grammar!

English speakers often use *Let's* . . . (Let's go. Let's finish the work.) because it's more polite than a command (Go! Finish the work!). You can make any command more polite by saying *please*. (Please sit down. Give me that book, please.)

B. Verbs with Infinitives

Verbs	Examples	Notes
hate	I **hate to clean** the house.	The infinitive is *to* + simple verb. Some sentences follow this pattern: Subject + verb 1 + infinitive (*to* + verb 2). The first verb can be in any tense. The second verb is always the simple form.
have	We **have to clean** the house today.	
know how	I **know how to do** laundry, but	
	I **don't know how to iron.**	
like	I **like to read.**	
love	I **love to listen** to music.	
need	We **need to do** the laundry.	
plan	I **plan to study** tonight.	
want	We **want to relax** this weekend.	

4   Use *want to* to make complete sentences about the children in the following pictures.

Example: become a doctor
          help sick people
          She wants to become a doctor.
          She wants to help sick people.

1. live in Paris
   be an artist

2. work very hard
   build bridges

3. open a restaurant
   become famous chefs

4. be very rich
   have lots and lots
   of money

5. be police officers
   stop drug dealers

5   Ask and answer questions with the following cues and *know how to*. Then add six questions of your own.

Example: make Middle Eastern food

   A.   Do you know how to make Middle Eastern food?

   B.   Yes, I do. I like to eat Middle Eastern food a lot.

   or No, I don't. I don't know how to cook!

1.   make Chinese food   7.   _____

2.   bake a cake   8.   _____

3.   iron   9.   _____

4.   play chess   10.   _____

5.   dance   11.   _____

6.   use a computer   12.   _____

6   Use these verbs to complete the following conversations. Use an infinitive in each sentence.

1.   **do   help   study   ✓ wash**

Rita: Ricky, you have ___*to wash*___ the dishes tonight.

Ricky: I don't want _____ the dishes, Mom. Besides, I need _____ my lesson.

Rita: You need _____ around the house too!

2.   **do   clean   cut   relax**

Steven: I don't like _____ housework.

Loretta: Well, I hate _____ the grass, but I cut it. Come on. We need _____ the windows.

Steven: OK. But then I want _____ all day.

7   Complete this conversation. Use the simple or the infinitive form of the verbs in parentheses.

James: Let's _go_ (go) to a movie tonight. I want _____ (see) *Superman VI.*

Marta: Well, we need _____ (find) a baby-sitter first.

James: _____ (call) my mother. She usually likes _____ (baby-sit) for her grandson. Alex likes _____ (play) at Grandma's house.

Marta: OK, but somebody needs _____ (do) the laundry first.

James: _____ (do) the laundry, and then let's _____ (go) to the movie.

Marta: Fine, but you have _____ (help) me.

James: Well, I don't really want _____ (do) laundry.

Marta: And I don't want _____ (see) *Superman VI.* Let's _____ (stay) home. Let's _____ (rent) videos.

James: Great idea! *Superman I, II, III, IV,* and *V*!

Using What You've Learned

8   **Telling People to Do Things.**   Look at the pictures. Give a command for each picture.

9   **Making Suggestions.**   Is it easy to learn English? Is it fun? Do you have some good ideas about learning English?

- Take turns making suggestions. Use *let's*. One person should write down the ideas for your group.
- Then as a class, compare all the suggestions. Who has the best ideas?

Examples: Let's invite some native English speakers to our class.
Let's meet outside of class to practice!

10 **Talking About Likes, Needs, and Wants.**   Take turns asking one another these questions.

1. Name two things you like to do. Name two things you don't like to do.
2. What are two things you need to do today? What are two things you have to do this week?
3. What do you want to do this evening? What do you plan to do this weekend?

PART 4

Contrast of Simple Present and Present Continuous Tenses; Nonaction Verbs; Object Pronouns

Setting the Context

Prereading Questions   Look at each picture. What are the people doing? Why?

Best Friends

Your best friend is your very special friend. Your best friend knows you well and understands you. You help each other, and you listen to each other. You tell each other the truth. You laugh together, and you cry together. You remember the good times, and you forget the bad times. You sometimes have fights, but you always love each other.

Check Your Understanding   Circle T for *True* or F for *False*.

1.   T F Your best friend rarely understands you.
2.   T F Friends tell each other the truth.
3.   T F Friends never cry.
4.   T F You never fight with a friend.

A. Simple Present Tense Versus Present Continuous Tense

	Examples	**Notes**
Simple Present Tense	I always **tell** my friends everything.	The simple present tense is used for facts, opinions, or repeated actions.
Present Continuous Tense	Right now he's **telling** a story to his friend.	The present continuous tense is used for actions that are happening now.

1   **Information Gap.**   Here are two charts with different information. One student looks only at Student A's chart. The other student looks only at Student B's chart. Ask a partner questions to complete your chart.

Example: B.   What is Sally doing now?
            A.   What does John do every Monday morning?

Student A			
	Now	*Every Monday Morning*	*Every Saturday Night*
Sally	sleep	_____	_____
Sam	_____	work at a restaurant	_____
John	eat a snack	_____	_____
Jane	_____	work in a hospital	visit family

Student B			
	Now	*Every Monday Morning*	*Every Saturday Night*
Sally	_____	baby-sit	work at a movie theatre
Sam	read a magazine	_____	go out with friends
John	_____	play tennis	stay home
Jane	take a nap	_____	_____

2 Complete these sentences. Use the simple present or the present continuous tense.

1. Right now my mother (or sister, brother, etc.) _____ .

2. On Friday nights, I _____ .

3. Our teacher always _____ .

4. My best friend often _____ .

5. At this moment, my friend _____ .

6. My friend and I never _____ .

7. On weekends I usually _____ .

8. Right now, my teacher _____ .

B. Nonaction Verbs

Feelings, Opinions, and Thoughts		
	Examples	**Notes**
be	I **am** his friend.	These verbs describe feelings and thoughts. They also describe things we own or possess. Because the verbs do not describe actions, they are used in the simple tenses (simple present, simple past, etc.). They are not generally used in the continuous tenses, even when the time is *now*.
forget	I **forget** his name.	
hate	They **hate** to be late.	
like	He **likes** to get together with old friends.	
love	They **love** their dog.	
mean	What **does** it **mean?**	
need	I **need** friends.	
remember	I don't **remember.**	
understand	I don't **understand** that word.	
want	I **want** to know.	

Possession		
	Examples	**Notes**
belong to	It **doesn't belong to** me.	See **Notes** section in the above chart. (See page 76 for more information on *have*.)
have	I **have** two close friends.	
own	I **own** an old car.	

3 Take turns asking and answering these questions.

1. Do you remember the first day of class?
2. Do you like Italian food?
3. Do you understand the news on TV?
4. Do you need to spend time alone?
5. Do you own a car?
6. Does this book belong to you?

7. Do you know what "cyberspace" means?

8. Do you want to go home now?

4   Complete these questions.

1. Do you remember _____?

2. Do you like _____?

3. Do you understand _____?

4. Do you need _____?

5. Do you own _____?

6. Does your teacher have _____?

7. Do your friends like _____?

8. Does your family love _____?

Take turns asking your questions and answering your classmate's questions.

C. Have—*Simple Present Versus Present Continuous Tense*

Possession		
	Examples	**Notes**
have	I **have** a new car. She **has** a headache.	Use the simple present tense to show possession.

Other Expressions		
	Examples	**Notes**
have a problem	I**'m having a problem** with my boyfriend.	Use the present continuous tense for actions happening now.
have a good time	They**'re having a good time** at the party.	
have a party	She**'s having a party** at her apartment right now.	
have breakfast (lunch, dinner, etc.)	We**'re having a snack** because we're hungry.	

5   Complete these sentences with *have / has* or *am / is / are having*.

1. I <u> have </u> a car. I <u> am having </u> problems with my car.

2. I _____ a party right now. Come on over.

3. I _____ a headache. I'm sorry, but I can't come.

4. I _____ no friends here.

5. I _____ a problem with this question.

6. My friend _____ a close friend—me!

7. Who _____ my grammar book?

D. Pronouns and Possessive Adjectives

Subject Pronouns		Possessive Adjectives		Object Pronouns	
Singular	**Plural**	**Singular**	**Plural**	**Singular**	**Plural**
I	we	my	our	me	us
you	you	your	your	you	you
he	they	his	their	him	them
she		her		her	
it		its		it	

Object Pronouns					
Form			**Subject + verb + object (object pronoun)**		
I	love	my	mother.	=	I	love	her.
He	loves	English.		=	He	loves	it.
He	loves	his teachers.		=	He	loves	them.

6 Change the words in parentheses to object pronouns.

1. I often write to my girlfriend. I write to _____*her*_____ every week.

2. My mother is old. I always help (my mother) _____.

3. My cousin and his wife live in Vancouver. I often visit (my cousin and his wife)

    _____.

4. We are a nice class. Don't forget (all the people in this class) _____.

5. My grandfather lives in a small village. I often think about (my grandfather)

    _____.

6. Where is my grammar book? Oh, no! I lost (my grammar book)

    _____.

7. It's our grammar teacher's birthday. I have a present for (our grammar teacher)

    _____.

8. Every Sunday my parents call. Every Wednesday I call (my parents)

    _____.

9. My friends are not here. I miss (my friends) _____.

7 Circle the correct pronouns in these readings.

1. My best friend is my husband. He always understands (I / my / me) problems. He always asks (I / my / me) for opinions. He respects (I / my / me). People are always happy to see (we / our / us) together. After 40 years of marriage, (he / his / him) is still my best friend, and I still love (he / his / him).

2. My best friend is (I / my / me) computer, Mac. I spend six to ten hours a day with (it / its). A computer is really a great friend. I always tell (it / its) what to do. Sometimes it doesn't understand (I / my / me). Then (we / our / us) spend hours together. We try to communicate. We try to solve (we / our / us) problems. In the end, (we / our / us) always find an answer. I appreciate Mac.

3. Hi! (I / My / Me) am Chris Hill. My best friend is my dog, Honey. (She / Her) is a good dog. I love (she / her). She follows (I / my / me) everywhere. I'm never lonely. Every day my friends come over, and (she / her) plays with (they / their / them). Someday she will have puppies. My friends each want one of (she / her) puppies.

8 Use the simple present tense to complete this reading.

My Best Friend

I __*have*__ (have) a best friend. My best friend _____ (be) a very special person, and I _____ (love) her very much. We _____ (have / always) fun together. She _____ (know) me and she _____ (understand) me very well.

Now my friend _____ (live) far away. This _____ (mean) we
_____ (not see) each other very often. We _____ (have) to write letters
and e-mails to each other. I _____ (like) to read her letters and e-mails because
she _____ (tell / always) interesting stories.

I _____ (feel / sometimes) lonely because she _____ (be) far away. I
_____ (miss) her very much. But today I _____ (feel) very happy because
she is going to come for a visit. I _____ (be) very excited.

Using What You've Learned

9   **Writing About Friends.**   Write a short paragraph about a friend. Why is your friend
special? What do you do together? Where is your friend now? What is he or she doing?

_____

_____

_____

_____

_____

_____

_____

_____

_____

_____

_____

_____

_____

_____

_____

_____

_____

_____

_____

_____

_____

Video Activities: Pet Behavior

Before You Watch.

1. Which of these animals are common pets?

    a. dog   b. lion   c. cat   d. chicken

2. What is an animal shelter for?

    a. sick pets   b. bad pets   c. homeless pets

Watch.

1. What was the dog owner's problem?
    a. The dogs ate a lot.
    b. The dogs were noisy.
    c. The dogs destroyed things.

2. What was the dogs' problem?
    a. They were bored.
    b. They were afraid.
    c. They were hungry.

3. What is Emily's business?
    a. She adopts dogs.
    b. She teaches dogs.
    c. She visits dogs.

4. What do most dogs need?
    a. Other dogs.
    b. A lot of toys.
    c. People's attention.

5. Everyone who adopts a dog from the animal shelter promises to
    a. spend time with the dog.
    b. send the dog to school.
    c. hire Emily.

Watch Again.

1. What are the dogs' names?

    _____ Weiner   _____ Arnold

    _____ Max   _____ Taylor

    _____ Otis

2. Check the things that the dogs damaged.

    _____ couch   _____ fireplace

    _____ coffee table   _____ curtains

    _____ bed   _____ chair

    _____ carpet   _____ table

After You Watch.

Unscramble the sentences. Put the words in the correct order.

1. usually like dogs people spend to time with
2. often destroy dogs bored things
3. their to owners animals play need with pets
4. hate home dogs be to alone usually

Chapter 4

Health Care

Modal Auxiliaries: *Can* and *Can't;* Yes/No Questions; Questions with *When, Where,* and *How*

Setting the Context

Prereading Questions   Look at the picture of a father and son below. In your opinion, how old is the father? How old does he look?

Getting Dad to the Gym

Ted: When are you going to start taking care of yourself, Dad?
Dad: I can't. I'm too old.
Ted: You can! It's never too late. You can change your eating habits and start exercising.
Dad: Where can I exercise? I can't go to the gym. I'm too embarrassed. I look too fat.
Ted: How can you say that, Dad? There are a lot of heavy or overweight people at the gym. They're trying to get into shape.
Dad: I can't go there. I really can't.
Ted: Well, then you can walk outside or in the mall.
Dad: Son, I can't reach the TV. Please change the channel and pass me another bag of potato chips.

Check Your Understanding

1.   Why does Ted worry about his father?
2.   Does Ted's father want to go to the gym? Why or why not?
3.   Do you think Ted's father will start exercising?

A. Modal Auxiliaries

The modal auxiliaries are *can, could, may, might, must, ought to, shall, should, will,* and *would.* These are special verb forms in English. They do not change forms; they do not add *-s* or *-ed.* They change meaning. Each word has several different meanings.

Expressing Present Abilities—*Can* and *Can't (Cannot)*			
Form	**Subject + *can* + verb**	**Subject + *can't* (*cannot*) + verb**	
	Affirmative	**Negative**	**Notes**
I You He She It We They	**can run** fast.	I You He She It We They **can't swim.** **cannot swim.**	*Can* and *can't* (*cannot*) are used to tell about abilities. The simple form of a verb always follows *can, can't,* and other modal auxiliaries.

1 Underline all uses of *can* and *can't* in the conversation on page 82.

2 Some people like to play sports for physical fitness. Which sports do you play? Make sentences with *can* or *can't*.

Example: swim
             I can swim.
             or I can't swim.

1. run a mile
2. do aerobics
3. play soccer
4. ski
5. play volleyball
6. play tennis
7. lift weights
8. skate
9. play baseball
10. swim
11. dive
12. play basketball

B. Yes/No Questions and Short Answers

Yes/No Questions		**Possible Answers**	
Form	***Can* + subject + *verb***	**Affirmative** **Subject + *can***	**Negative** **Subject + *can't***
Can	I you he she it we they **swim** here?	Yes, I you he she it we they **can.**	No, I you he she it we they **can't.**

3 Use *can* to make questions about these actions. Take turns asking and answering the questions.

Example: walk ten miles
          A.   Can you walk ten miles?
          B.   Yes, I can.
             or No, I can't.

1. touch your toes
2. lift 50 pounds
3. run a mile
4. change a flat tire
5. cook Chinese food
6. dance the tango
7. play the piano
8. read Italian
9. sing well
10. ride a bicycle ten miles
11. do six push-ups
12. do three chin-ups
13. water ski
14. speak Russian
15. use a computer
16. whistle
17. _____
18. _____

4 In negative statements, people often use *don't* or *doesn't know how to* instead of *can't* or *cannot*. Make sentences with *can* and *not know how to* about the following people.

Example: *He can swim, but he doesn't
know how to water-ski.*

C. Questions with *When and* Where

Form	Question + *can* + subject + *verb*			
Information Questions				**Possible Answers**
When can	we	**swim**	here?	After 4:30.
Where can	he	**buy**	a bicycle?	At City Sports Store.

D. Questions with How

Form	*How* + adverb + *can* + subject + verb		
Information Questions	**Possible Answers**	**Notes**	
How far How fast **can you run?** How long	I can run three miles. I can't run very fast! I can't run for very long. I can run for about 15 minutes.	*How far . . .?* asks about distance. *How fast . . .?* asks about speed. *How long . . .?* asks about length or period of time. *For +* period of time is often used in answers.	

5   Write questions for the answers. Then take turns asking and answering.

Example: A.   *How far can you walk?*   (walk)

B.   I can walk five miles easily!

1.   _____ (run)

Not far at all!

2.   _____ (ride your bicycle)

Not very fast at all!

3.   _____ (ski)

Too fast!

4.   _____ (hold 100 pounds)

Not long at all!

5.   _____ (throw a football)

Really far!

6.   _____ (swim)

Not very far!

Using What You've Learned

6   **Information Gap.**   Use question words and *can I* to make questions using the cues on page 86. Then take turns asking and answering the questions.

■ Student A should cover up Student B's answers.

■ Student B should cover up Student A's questions.

Example: where / play tennis at the high school

        A.   Where can I play tennis?

        B.   You can play tennis at the high school.

Student A	Student B
1. where / buy running shoes	at any shoe store
2. where / play basketball	at the high school
3. when / use the swimming pool	from 7:00 A.M. to 7:00 P.M.
4. where / rent a bicycle	at a bike shop
5. when / go to aerobics class	at 6:00 P.M.
6. how / learn to dive	take lessons
7. where / buy a basketball	at the sports store
8. where / play volleyball	at the beach
9. how / skate well	practice a lot
10. where / surf	in Hawaii

7   **Giving and Getting Information.**   Think of six interesting questions to ask other students.

■ Write three questions with *where can I . . . ?* and three with *when can I . . . ?*

■ Then ask six people your questions.

Examples: *Where can I find good Japanese food?*
                   When can I have lunch with you?

8   **Talking About Activities.**   What sports can you play? What languages can you speak, read, or write?

■ Work in a small group. Take turns asking and answering questions with *can*. Use the following ideas and add categories and activities of your own.

■ Then, make a chart on the board. How many people can do each game, hobby, or sport?

Games	Hobbies	Sports	
play checkers	cook	bowl	_____
play chess	knit	play golf, soccer, etc.	_____
_____	make furniture	skate	_____
_____	play a musical instrument	_____	_____

<table>
<tr><td>**PART 2**</td></tr>
</table>

Could and *Would* with Requests and Desires

Setting the Context

Prereading Questions   Look at this picture. What problem does the man have? Who is he calling for help?

A Bad Toothache

Receptionist: Good afternoon. Could you hold please? *[click]* Thank you for holding. Can I help you?
Alex: Yes, thank you. I would like to make a dental appointment.
Receptionist: Is this for a checkup?
Alex: No, it's an emergency! I would like to see the dentist today. I have a bad toothache.
Receptionist: Is 4:30 OK?
Alex: Could I come at 5:00? I have to work until 4:30.

Receptionist: The last appointment is at 4:45. Can you come then?
Alex: Yes. I need help! See you at 4:45, and thanks!

Discussion Questions

1.   Why does Alex need to see the dentist?
2.   Can he see the dentist at 5:00?
3.   What time is his appointment?

A. Making Requests for Permission

Form	*Could* + *I* or *we* + verb		
Questions	**Possible Answers**		**Notes**
	Affirmative	**Negative**	
Could I make a 5:00 appointment?	Yes, of course.	No, our last appointment is at 4:45.	In these cases, we want to do something and are asking for someone's help or permission.
Could we talk to Dr. Smith?	Sure. (informal)	Sorry, but she isn't here.	

Note: Be careful with the pronunciation of *could.* Do not pronounce the *l. Could* rhymes with *good.*

1 Use *could I* to make requests. Answer with *Yes, of course,* or *I'm sorry, s/he isn't here now.*

Example: see the doctor

Could I see the doctor, please? Yes, of course.

B. Making Requests for Action

Questions	Possible Answers		Notes
	Affirmative	**Negative**	
Could + { you / he / she / it / they } + verb			
Could you help me, please? **Could they help** me?	Certainly. No problem! (informal)	Sorry, but I can't. Sorry, it's not possible.	In these cases, we are asking someone else to do something.

2 Use *could you* to make requests. Use answers from the chart above.

Example: find a Band-Aid

Could you find a Band-Aid, please?
No problem!

1. help me
2. give me some information
3. fill this prescription for me
4. explain these instructions

5. tell me the meaning of this word
6. get me some water please
7. give me a bigger bottle
8. recommend something for mosquito bites

C. Expressing Desires and Making Requests

Statements with Nouns	Statements with Infinitives	Notes
Subject + *would like* + **noun**	**Subject** + *would like* + **infinitive**	
I would like some aspirin.	We **would like to buy** some aspirin, please.	*Would like* is used to tell our desires and to make requests. It is more polite than *want to*.
I'd also **like** some cold medicine.	**We'd** also **like to get** some cold medicine.	The contracted form of *would* is *'d*

Note: Be careful with the pronunciation of *would*. Do not pronounce the *l. Would* rhymes with *good*.

3   Use the pictures to make statements with *would like to.*

Example: buy

I would like to buy some aspirin, please.

Chiropractic treatments involve adjusting the spine, usually to relieve pain. For years, many people did not believe this could help them. Today there are thousands of chiropractors. Many insurance companies now pay for chiropractic visits.

D. Questions

Questions	Possible Answers	
Would + subject + *like* + noun or infinitive	**Affirmative**	**Negative**
Would you like some dinner?	Yes, please.	No, thank you.
Would you like to go out for lunch?	Yes, of course.	Sorry, but I can't today.

4   Work with a partner. Ask and answer questions. Use *would you like to . . . ?* with the following cues. Give true answers.

Example: learn CPR (cardiopulmonary resuscitation)
       A.   Would you like to learn CPR?
       B.   Yes, it's very important.

1.   change your eating habits
2.   learn first aid
3.   learn how to ski
4.   take a nap
5.   travel around the world
6.   open a business someday
7.   have a massage
8.   go home now

Using What You've Learned

5   **Making Requests.**   Ask other students for something—anything! Go around your group making requests and responding to them. Continue asking until everyone has had a turn.

Example: A.   Could you help me with my homework?
       B.   Sure I could. Could you buy me a soda?
       C.   Sorry, but I don't have my wallet with me.

6   **Making Requests.**   Role play these telephone conversations. Then create one of your own.

1.   You want to make a dental appointment for a checkup. Call the dentist's office.
2.   You have a bad toothache, and you would like to make an emergency appointment with the dentist. Call the dentist's office.
3.   You want to make an appointment with your doctor for a yearly checkup. Call the doctor's office.
4.   You need a prescription for antibiotics. Ask the pharmacist.
5.   Your back hurts. Call the chiropractor for an appointment.
6.   You want to stop smoking. Ask your doctor for help.
7.   You want a massage. Call the spa for an appointment.
8.   You want to get in shape. Ask the trainer at the gym for help.

PART 3	*Should, Must, and Have to*

Setting the Context

Prereading Questions   Look at the picture. Is this a serious accident? Why is the police officer writing a ticket?

A Car Accident

Misha is driving in the U.S. with his daughter, Yuliya. Yuliya is only two years old, but she is not sitting in a car seat. She is not even wearing a seat belt. A car turns in front of Misha, and he has to stop quickly. Yuliya hits her head, but she is not hurt seriously.   5

Now the other driver is getting out of his car. What should Misha do? He doesn't know. Then a policewoman stops. She is angry at Misha. "Do you have insurance? You must keep insurance in-   10
formation in your car! Where is your child's car seat? You must not drive without a car seat! You should know this. I am going to give you a ticket."

Misha is lucky because Yuliya isn't hurt. But Misha is very upset. He will put his insurance in-   15
formation in the car today, and he is going to buy a car seat, too.

Check Your Understanding   Circle T for *True* or F for *False*.

1.   T F Misha knows all the U.S. driving laws very well.
2.   T F Misha needs to buy a car seat for his daughter.
3.   T F Misha has to pay money for his mistake.
4.   T F Misha is going to keep his birth certificate in his car.

A. Giving Advice

Affirmative **Subject + *should* + verb**		**Negative** **Subject +** *should not* *shouldn't* **+ verb**		**Notes**
You He She It We They	**should go** now.	You He She It We They	**should not stay.** **shouldn't stay.**	Use *should* and *should not* to give advice. The simple form of a verb follows *should* and other modal auxiliaries.

Note: Be careful with the pronunciation of *should*. Do not pronounce the *l. Should* rhymes with *good.*

1   Underline the uses of *should* in the reading above.

2 What should you do in an emergency? What shouldn't you do? Here is a short test for you. First, complete these sentences with *should* or *shouldn't*. Then, in a small group, compare your answers. Do you all agree? Finally, as a group, write one original sentence for each situation.

1. You are walking down the street, and you see a bad car accident. People are seriously hurt. You _should_ call for help. You _should_ call the police or 911, the emergency telephone number in many parts of the United States. You _shouldn't_ walk away.
   Sentence: _You should try to help_.

2. There is a fire in your apartment building. You _____ use the elevator. If there is a lot of smoke, you _____ try to run down the hall. You _____ try to take all your things with you.
   Sentence: _____

3. A pregnant woman _____ drink alcohol or smoke. She _____ see a doctor early in her pregnancy. She _____ continue to eat a healthy diet.
   Sentence: _____

4. Carlos doesn't understand the safety rules for his job. He _____ ask his supervisor or a friend for a translation. He _____ pretend to understand because he is embarrassed.
   Sentence: _____

5. Lidia has trouble sleeping. She _____ drink a lot of caffeinated drinks before bedtime. She _____ take sleeping pills every night. She _____ talk to her friends. She _____ go to a doctor.
   Sentence: _____

3 Look at the chart about emergency situations below. Read the information and check the important vocabulary. Then change each command to a statement with *should* or *should not*.

Example: If possible, check the victim for injuries.
     If possible, you should check the victim for injuries.

Vocabulary

artificial respiration = forcing air into someone who is not breathing
injury = a hurt or wound
rescue = to save someone from danger
unconscious = not awake
victim = someone who is hurt

> # Emergency First Aid
> 1. Call for medical help immediately. (Dial 911.)
> 2. If possible, check the victim for injuries.
> 3. Do not move the victim if it is not necessary.
> 4. If a rescue is necessary, move the victim
>   quickly and carefully.
> 5. Check for breathing.
> 6. Give artificial respiration if necessary.
> 7. Control bleeding.
> 8. Do not give food or drink to an unconscious victim.

911 is the phone number people use in emergencies in most parts of the United States. If you dial 911, the operator will automatically know your phone number and location. That way, help can be sent to you even if you cannot speak.

B. Expressing Needs or Obligations

Affirmative	Negative	
Subject + *must* + verb	**Subject + *must not* + verb**	*Must* and *must not* are strong expressions. They show that something is very important or necessary. *Must not* also shows that something is not allowed.
I You He She **must be** careful It We They	I You He She **must not** do that. It We They	

4   Use the cues below to make sentences with *must* or *must not*. Compare your answers in a small group. Write an original sentence for each situation

Example: keep the building clean
      The landlord must keep the building clean.

1.   If you rent an apartment, the landlord must or must not do this:
   a.   keep the building clean
   b.   provide smoke alarms
   c.   enter your apartment without your permission
   d.   make repairs quickly
   e.   rent to people of any color or religion
   f.   _____

2.   If you drive a car, you must or must not do this:
   a.   use a car seat for young children
   b.   bring your license with you

    c. keep your car registration and insurance information in the car

    d. drive with six or more people in a compact car

    e. _____

3. If you have small children, you must or must not do this:

    a. leave them home alone, even for a short time

    b. use car seats for them

    c. leave medicine or cleaning supplies around the house

    d. get immunizations for them

    e. _____

5 Read this label from a bottle of cold medicine. The label uses difficult vocabulary, but the information is important. Use a dictionary to look up difficult words. Then look at each pair of sentences below the label. Circle the letter of the sentence with the correct meaning.

All Night Cold Medicine

WARNING: Use this product ONLY as directed. Do not exceed the recommended dosage. Do not use this product for more than seven days. If your condition does not improve, consult a doctor. Do not take this product if you have heart disease or diabetes. Avoid alcoholic beverages while you are taking this product. Use caution when driving a motor vehicle or using machinery.

    5

---

1. Use this product ONLY as directed.

    (a.) You must follow the directions for this medicine.

    b. You don't need to read the directions.

2. Do not exceed the recommended dosage.

    a. You can take any amount of medicine.

    b. You must take the correct amount of medicine for your age or weight.

3. Do not use this product for more than seven days.

    a. You must not take this medicine for more than a week.

    b. You must take this medicine for a week.

4. If your condition does not improve, consult a doctor.

    a. If you get better, you should talk to a doctor.

    b. If you do not feel better, you should talk to a doctor.

5. Do not take this product if you have heart disease or diabetes.

    a. If you have heart problems or diabetes, you must not use this medicine.

    b. You must use this medicine if you have heart problems or diabetes.

6. Avoid alcoholic beverages while you are taking this product.

    a. You can take this medicine and drink beer or wine at the same time.

    b. You must not take this medicine and drink beer or wine at the same time.

7. Use caution when driving a motor vehicle or using machinery.

    a. You must be very careful when you are driving or using a machine.

    b. You can drive or use a machine and take this medicine at the same time without any problems.

C. Have to *and* Must

	Examples	Notes
have to **must**	You **have to use** a car seat with small children. You **must use** a car seat with small children.	In affirmative statements, *have to* and *must* are very similar in meaning.

6   Rewrite the sentences below. Use *have to* or *has to* in each new sentence.

Example: Misha must buy a car seat for his daughter.
Misha has to buy a car seat for his daughter.

1.   Misha must pay his ticket.

_____

2.   You must drive carefully at all times.

_____

3.   You must obey the speed limits.

_____

4.   Young children must sit in car seats.

_____

5.   You must read the instructions on medicine bottles.

_____

6.   Children must have immunizations.

_____

7.   Your landlord must put smoke alarms in your building.

_____

8.   You must observe the no smoking rules.

_____

In many places around the world there are smoking restrictions in public places. In some places you cannot smoke inside buildings, including restaurants and bars. Do you think this is a good idea?

D. Don't / Doesn't have to *Versus* Must not

	Examples	Notes
don't/doesn't have to **must not**	Adults **don't have to use** car seats. You **must not drive** without a license.	*Don't/Doesn't have to* means "It is not necessary." *Must not* has a very different meaning. *Must not* means "it is not allowed." There is no choice.

7 Check the correct statements.

Example: ☐ You don't have to drink and drive.
            ☑ You must not drink and drive.

1.   ☐ You don't have to carry an umbrella in the rain.
     ☐ You must not carry an umbrella in the rain.
2.   ☐ You don't have to put a knife in a toaster.
     ☐ You must not put a knife in a toaster.
3.   ☐ You don't have to drive without a seat belt.
     ☐ You must not drive without a seat belt.
4.   ☐ You don't have to keep your birth certificate in your car.
     ☐ You must not keep your birth certificate in your car.
5.   ☐ You don't have to take the TOEFL to enter some U.S. colleges.
     ☐ You must not take the TOEFL to enter some U.S. colleges.

Using What You've Learned

8 **Explaining Rules.**   It's important to "know the rules" in a new situation. Sometimes there are specific rules or even laws, and we must or must not do some things. Other things are important to do (or not to do), but we have a choice.

■ Think about the following three situations. Write rules for each situation.
■ Explain the rules to the class.

	Must	**Should**	**Doesn't have to**
A visitor in any country	obey the laws	try to speak the language	carry a birth certificate
A student in this program A person in an emergency situation			

Examples: A visitor in any country must obey the laws.
            A visitor in any country should try to speak the language.
            A visitor in any country doesn't have to carry a birth certificate.

9 **Talking About Emergency Situations.**   Talk about first aid in a real situation. Take turns asking and answering these questions.

Example: You see and smell a fire in the house next door. What should you do?
            You should call the fire department or 911. Then you should get outside quickly.

1.   You see a bad car accident. What should you do first?
2.   The people in the car have injuries. Should you move them?
3.   The car is starting to burn. Should you move the victims?
4.   One person is not breathing. Should you try to give the person water? What should you do?
5.   One person is bleeding a lot. What should you do?

| PART 4 | *Might* with Possibilities; Using *Or;* Simple Future Tense with *Will* |

Setting the Context

Prereading Questions   In this picture, some friends are playing soccer. What is happening?

Call 911

Alfonso: Ohhh . . . My leg . . .
Frank: What's the matter? Are you OK? What hurts?
Alfonso: My left leg . . . My ankle . . .
Ali: His ankle might be sprained, or it might be broken.
Alvaro: How far is the hospital? Let's take him there.
Keizo: We shouldn't move him. That might make it worse. I'll call 911 right now.
Bedi: Let's find a phone. It won't take long for someone to come, will it?
Alvaro: Don't worry, Alfonso. You'll be OK. Help will be here in a minute. We'll take good care of you.

Check Your Understanding

1. Who is hurt?
2. What might be wrong with his leg?
3. Are his friends going to take him to the hospital? If not, what are they going to do?

A. Expressing Present and Future Possibilities

Affirmative	Negative	Notes
Subject + *might* + **verb** I You He She ⎫ **might stay here.** It ⎬ We They ⎭	**Subject** + *might not* + **verb** I You He She ⎫ **might not leave.** It ⎬ We They ⎭	*Might* means "maybe," "perhaps," or "possibly." *Might* is rarely used in questions. The simple form of a verb follows *might* and other modal auxiliaries.

1 Underline the uses of *might* in the conversation on page 97. Circle the verb after each.

2 Read these statements, and make statements with *might*. Use the cues in parentheses.

Example: It's cloudy today. (rain)
  It might rain.

1. It's winter in Alaska. It's very cold and cloudy. (snow)
2. It's summer in Miami. It's very hot and cloudy. (storm)
3. She isn't in class today. (be sick)
4. He is sick, and he feels hot and cold. (have a fever)
5. She's only eating salad and yogurt. (be on a diet)
6. I never see him eat meat. (be a vegetarian)
7. She cries often. (be homesick)
8. They speak two languages. (be bilingual)

B. Using Or

	Examples	Notes
Two Sentences	I might go to the library. I might go shopping.	*Or* can join two sentences. In writing, use a comma before *or*.
One Sentence	I might go to the library, **or** I might go shopping..	

3 Look at the pictures on the next page. What alternatives are these people thinking about? Make sentences with *might* and *or*.

Example: *She might stay on her diet,*
            or she might have an ice cream cone.

C. The Simple Future Tense

Affirmative	Negative	Notes
Subject + *will* + verb	Subject + *will not* + verb *won't*	*Will* is used to talk about the future. People also use *will* to make offers, predictions, promises, and requests.
I You He She **will be** here soon. It We They	I You He She **will not be** late. It **won't be** late. We They	

4 We often use *will* or *won't* to make promises. Imagine you are going away from home for the first time. You are talking to your parents. Use the following cues to make promises with *will* or *won't*. Then add two more promises.

Example: eat healthy food

I promise I will eat healthy food, Mom.

1. eat breakfast every day _____
2. get a lot of sleep _____
3. not go to many parties _____
4. get some excercise every week _____

5. not watch soap operas _____

6. read more books _____

7. do the laundry _____

8. not call collect _____

9. _____

10. _____

D. Questions and Answers

Statement	She will study for the test.	Possible Answers
Yes / No Questions	**Will** + **subject** + **verb** **Will** she **study** for the test?	Yes, she will. No, she won't.
Information **Questions**	**Question word** + **will** + **subject** + **verb** **When** **will** she **study?** **Where** **will** she **study?**	Tonight. At home.

5 People often use *will* to make requests. Imagine you and your partner are very good friends. Both of you are moving to new places, and you are saying good-bye. Take turns making requests and giving responses. Use the cues below and add two original requests.

Example: write soon

  A.   Will you write soon?

  B.   Of course. I promise I will.

1. call me from time to time
2. take care of yourself
3. have a good time
4. be careful
5. remember all of us
6. keep in touch
7. _____
8. _____

6 Two old friends meet each other on the street. Complete their conversation with the simple present or the simple future tense. Add negatives when indicated.

Jane: Hi, Susan. How _are_ (be) you? You _look_ (look) great!

Susan: Well, I _____ (work) at the health club, and I _____ (get) a lot of ex-
                        1   2
ercise. I _____ (teach) aerobics classes there.
                3

Jane: _____ you _____ (like it)?
          4   5

Susan: Yes, I _____ (like) it very much because my job _____ (be) fun, and
it _____ (keep) me in good shape. It _____ (be) a great combination.

Jane: I _____ (not get) any exercise, and I _____ (need) to change that. I
_____ (want) to look good—like you! _____ you _____ (be) there
tomorrow? I _____ (come) and _____ (register) for a class.

Susan: Come in the morning. I _____ (not be) there in the afternoon. OK? I
_____ (see) you tomorrow!

7 Jane enrolls in Susan's health club. Complete this conversation by circling the correct
modal.

Jane: I (can / can't / could) do this! I (can't / must / should) exercise anymore.
Susan: Yes, you (would / can / should)! You (would / will / should) try harder!
Jane: (Would / Could / Must) I stop for a minute? Whew! I (will / would / could / must)
like to die.
Susan: (Would / Could / Will) you like to take a break? You know, Jane, you
(would / could / should) get more exercise. Next time you (must / won't / will) feel
much better.
Jane: I (must / won't / can't) be here next time because I (must / will / can't) be in the
hospital!

Using What You've Learned

8 **Asking Questions.**

■ Take turns asking and answering these questions. Give true answers.
■ Use *be going to* for specific plans. Use *might* for possible plans.
■ Then add one question each.

Example: A. What are you going to do after class?
             B. I might go to the library, or I might go home.
                 or I am going to go to the library.

STUDENT A

1. What are you going to do tonight?
2. What are you going to wear tomorrow?
3. Where are you going to spend your next vacation?
4. _____

STUDENT B

1. What are you going to have for dinner?
2. Where are you going to go tomorrow night?
3. What are you going to do next weekend?
4. _____

9   **Pantomiming.**   One student thinks of a word. The student acts out the meaning *without speaking*. The other students try to guess the word. Look at the ideas below and add some of your own. Use *might* in your guesses.

Jobs	Animals	Athletes	Illnesses or Injuries
carpenter	cat	basketball player	the flu
doctor	elephant	golfer	a headache
pilot	lion	soccer player	a stomachache
plumber	tiger	tennis player	a toothache

Example: A: Keizo might be a plumber.
              B: He might be a carpenter.
              C: No! I know! He's a doctor.

10   **Making Offers.**   Make an offer other students cannot refuse.

- Go around your group in a chain. One student makes an offer.
- The next student responds and then makes an offer.
- The third student responds, and so on. Continue around your circle three times.
- Some possible responses are listed below.

Example: A: I'll give you a ride home.
              B: Great! I'll cook dinner for you tonight.

Possible Responses		
	Affirmative	**Negative**
Formal	Thank you very much.	I'm sorry, but . . .
Informal	Thanks a lot! Great! Sure thing!	Thanks, but no thanks. No way! Nothing doing!

11   **Making Predictions.**   Write your name on a piece of paper. Your teacher will collect the papers in a bag. Choose one name, but do not say it out loud. Use *will* or *won't* to write five predictions about that student's future. Your teacher will collect the predictions and then read them aloud. You do not have to sign your name.

Example: *Abdullah will become famous because he will be the star of an international TV program. He'll be very rich, but he won't forget about us. He'll invite us all to his home in Beverly Hills.*

Checking Your Progress

Check your progress with structures from Chapters 3 and 4. Be sure to review any problem areas.

Part 1. Choose the correct word(s) to complete each sentence.

1. I _____ a problem.
    a. has
    b. are
    c. take
    d. having
    e. have

2. Sue _____ the dishes at night.
    a. does
    b. do
    c. wash
    d. is
    e. doing

3. Penny _____.
    a. can't sleeping
    b. can't sleeps
    c. can't sleep
    d. cannot sleeps
    e. can't to sleep

4. Who _____ the house?
    a. does cleans
    b. does clean
    c. cleans
    d. clean
    e. cleaning

5. Marina usually _____ cook.
    a. is not to
    b. do not
    c. don't
    d. not
    e. doesn't

6. Could you _____ me please!
    a. to help
    b. helped
    c. helps
    d. helping
    e. help

7. I would _____.
    a. like to come
    b. to come
    c. liked to come
    d. like to came
    e. liking to come

8. Every night Joe _____ eight hours.
    a. to sleep
    b. is slept
    c. sleep
    d. sleeps
    e. is sleeping

9. I _____ hot dogs.
    a. hate
    b. am hating
    c. hates
    d. am
    e. to hate

10. Misha has _____ for his ticket.
    a. to pay
    b. pays
    c. to paid
    d. not paying
    e. pay

Part 2. Circle the correct words to complete this story. Circle "X" to show that nothing is necessary.

My family is very important to me. (Mine/My) mother died three years ago. I
$\qquad$ 1

(live/am live) with my father and two older brothers. I (love/am loving) them very
$\qquad$ 2 $\qquad$ 3

much. Every day I (make/makes) breakfast for the family. My father (eating/eats) a
$\qquad$ 4 $\qquad$ 5

big breakfast. He shouldn't (drink/drinks) four cups of coffee!
$\qquad$ 6

My older brother (has/is) 23 years old. He (working/works) for a computer con-
$\qquad$ 7 $\qquad$ 8

sulting company. He (usually works/works usually) ten to twelve hours a day. He
$\qquad$ 9

would like (to take/taking) a vacation but he (doesn't have to/can't) now. But he
$\qquad$ 10 $\qquad$ 11

(should/might) sleep more! He works very hard, like our father.
$\qquad$ 12

Video Activities: Brain Surgery

Before You Watch.

1. When a doctor has to fix a heart, what does he or she do?

    a. an examination   b. a transplant   c. surgery

2. What part of your body controls movement?

    a. your eyes   b. your heart   c. your brain   d. your leg

Watch.

1. What is this a picture of?

    a. a brain   b. a heart   c. a hand

2. Check the ways that Dr. Francel's surgery is different from others.

    _____ It's faster.   _____ He uses computers.

    _____ It's cheaper.   _____ He operates on brains.

3. Before the surgery, Mr. Previt's hand _____.

    a. hurt   b. couldn't move   c. shook

4. During the surgery, Mr. Previt is _____.

    a. sleeping   b. awake   c. shaking

5. After the surgery, Mr. Previt _____.

    a. can hold a glass   b. cannot feel his hand   c. can talk better

Watch Again.

Complete the sentences with numbers from the box.

$1\frac{1}{2}$ to 2	12	100	2

1. Dr. Francel does this surgery in _____ hours.

2. Other doctors do this surgery in _____ hours.

3. Dr. Francel can operate on _____ patients in a day.

4. A human hair is about _____ microns thick.

After You Watch.

Complete the sentences with the correct modal.

1. Dr. Francel _____ operate very quickly.
        can   should   must

2. All doctors _____ use computers.
        should have to   would

3. Dr. Francel's surgery _____ take less time than in other hospitals.
        might   must   will

4. A brain surgeon _____ work very carefully.
        has to   might   could

5. If a surgeon is not careful, his patient _____ die.
        must   can't   might

Chapter 5

Men and Women

| **PART 1** | # Simple Past Tense of the Verb *Be*; Yes/No Questions; Information Questions; *There was/There were* |

Setting the Context

Prereading Questions   Look at the photos below. Guess what year each photograph is from.

The Good Old Days

I'm a very old man now, and things change. When I was young, everything was different. There weren't so many decisions to make. We were not as free as young people today. But there weren't as many problems. In a way, life was easier.

Take marriage, for example. Who were you going to marry? It was simple. Just ask your parents. They were happy to find a wife for you.

Of course, you could look for a wife yourself. But you and she couldn't just decide to marry. You had to ask your father and her father. They could say yes or no. They could decide. We couldn't.

You see? Everything was different.

5

Check Your Understanding   Circle T for *True* or F for *False*. Then correct the false sentences.

1.   T (F) In the past, everything was ~~the same~~. *different*
2.   T F You could look for a wife.
3.   T F You and she could decide to marry.

4.   T F You had to ask your mother and her mother.

5.   T F The fathers could say yes or no to the marriage.

A. Was *and* Were—*Affirmative and Negative Statements*

Affirmative	Negative		Notes
	Long Form	**Contraction**	
I **was** happy.	I **was not** sad.	I **wasn't** sad.	The verb *be* is different from other verbs in English. Do not use an auxiliary or helping verb to make negative sentences with the verb *be*.
You **were** happy.	You **were not** sad.	You **weren't** sad.	
He She } **was** happy. It	He She } **was not** sad. It	He She } **wasn't** sad. It	
We You } **were** happy. They	We You } **were not** sad. They	We You } **weren't** sad. They	

1   Use *was* or *were* to complete these sentences. Use contractions for the negatives.

I'm Christine. The man in the reading was my grandfather. To show you how things have changed in our culture, I'd like to tell you a little about my family history.

1.   My grandparents __were__ introduced in 1938. They _____ at a dance.

2.   My grandmother's name _____ Catherine. My grandfather's _____ Robert.

3.   My grandfather _____ a medical student. My grandmother _____ in high school.

4. My grandmother _____ quite young. She _____ seventeen. My grandfather _____ (not) as young. He _____ twenty-two.

5. They _____ (not) from the same city. My grandfather _____ from Philadelphia. My grandmother _____ from New York.

6. They _____ also from different backgrounds. My grandfather's family _____ Scandinavian. My grandmother's family _____ from Spain.

7. Even their religion _____ (not) the same.

8. Finally, her family _____ rich. His family _____ poor.

9. To them, these things _____ (not) important. They _____ in love!

B. Was *and* Were—*Yes/No Questions and Short Answers*

Questions	Short Answers		Notes
	Affirmative	**Negative**	
***Was* or *were* + subject**			The verb *be* is different from other verbs in English. Do not use an auxiliary or helping verb to make questions with the verb *be*.
Was I tired?	Yes, I **was.**	No, I **wasn't.**	
Were you late?	Yes, you **were.**	No, you **weren't.**	
Was { he / she / it } late?	Yes, { he / she / it } **was.**	No, { he / she / it } **wasn't.**	
Were { we / you / they } hungry?	Yes, { we / you / they } **were.**	No, { we / you / they } **weren't.**	

2   Ask and answer these questions about Christine's grandparents from Activity 1.

Example: A.   Were Catherine and Robert introduced at school?
   B.   No, they weren't.

1. Was Robert a medical student?
2. Were they from different backgrounds?
3. Was Catherine the same age as Robert?
4. Were they from the same city?
5. Was Robert from Philadelphia?
6. Was Catherine from Los Angeles?
7. Was Catherine a medical student?
8. Were both families rich?

3   Talk about your grandparents or parents. Use the questions in Activity 2, but change the names to your grandmother and grandfather or your mother and your father. Take turns asking and answering your new questions. Then make two more questions. Ask your partner these new questions.

C. Information Questions with Who

	Examples	Notes
Statement	Catherine's parents were from Spain.	
Yes/No Question	*Was* or *were* + subject **Were** Catherine's parents from Spain?	
Question with *Who*	*Who* + *was* + adjective, noun, or **phrase**. **Who was** from Spain?	Questions with *who* are normally singular.

D. Information Questions with When, Where, How long, *and* How old

	Examples	Possible Answers
Statement	They were married in New York in 1941.	
Yes/No Question	*Was* or *were* + subject **Were** they married in New York in 1941?	Yes, they were.
Information Question	*Question word* + *was* or *were* + subject **When were** they married? **Where were** they married?	They were married in 1941. They were married in New York.

4   Make questions from these statements. The answers to the questions are the underlined words.

Examples: <u>Robert</u> was a medical student.

Who was a medical student?

They were introduced in <u>1938</u>.

When were they introduced?

1. Robert and Catherine were <u>at a dance</u>.
2. Robert was from <u>Philadelphia</u>.
3. <u>Catherine</u> was from New York.
4. She was <u>seventeen</u>.
5. He was <u>twenty-two</u>.
6. <u>Robert's parents</u> were Scandinavian.
7. Her family was from <u>Spain</u>.
8. They were married in <u>1941</u>.

Marriage between people of different religions or cultural backgrounds was once unusual. Today, such marriages are much more common.

E. There was/There were—*Statements and Questions*

	Affirmative Statements	Negative Statements
With a Singular Noun	There was a problem.	There wasn't a problem.
With Plural Nouns	There were some problems.	There weren't many problems.

	Yes/No Questions	Possible Answers	
		Affirmative	**Negative**
With a Singular Noun	Was there a problem?	Yes, there was.	No, there wasn't.
With Plural Nouns	Were there some problems?	Yes, there were.	No, there weren't.

5   Use *was* or *were* to complete these sentences. Use contractions for the negatives.

1. The marriage was a bad idea. There ___*were*___ several reasons.

2. First, there _____ religious differences between Catherine and Robert.

3. There _____ problems with money.

4. There _____ (not) many jobs at that time.

5. There _____ even a bigger problem.

6. There _____ a huge war in Europe.

7. In the United States, there _____ many young men already in the military.

8. There _____ (not) much hope for an end to the war.

In the past, the U.S. government used a draft system to choose young men for the military. Today, there is no draft. The U.S. military has all volunteers.

Using What You've Learned

6   **Asking About Family Histories.**   Do you know about your family history?

■ Take turns asking and answering questions about your grandparents and parents.
■ Use these cues to make questions.
■ Then add some of your own.
■ Take notes and write a short paragraph about your partner's family.

Examples: parents / born in the same city
　　　　　　Were your parents born in the same city?
　　　　　　where / born
　　　　　　Where were they born?

1. when / born
2. rich or poor
3. when / married
4. how old (when they met)
5. (grand) mother younger than your (grand) father

PART 2

Simple Past Tense with Regular Verbs; Pronunciation and Spelling; Affirmative and Negative Statements; Questions

Setting the Context

Prereading Questions   In the past, men went to work and women stayed home. Look at this photo from the 1950s. What did the woman do during the day? What did the man do?

Changing Possibilities

In the 1950s and into the 1960s men and women lived very different lives. Most women stayed home and took care of the children. Men kissed their wives goodbye in the morning and went to 5 work. Men often worked long days. They stayed away from their families from early in the morning until late at night. Women didn't go to work. Who cleaned the house? Women did. Who cooked 10 everyday? Women did.

Maybe some women did not want to stay at home. Maybe they wanted to go to work. Not many women had careers at that time. Maybe some men wanted to stay home with their children. Men and 15 women did not have many choices at that time. After the 1960s, the possibilities changed.

Check Your Understanding

1. What did most men do in the 1950s?
2. What did most women do in the 1950s?
3. Did most women work?
4. Did many men stay home with their children?

A. Simple Past Tense of Regular Verbs—Affirmative Statements

Form	Subject + verb + *-ed*		
Singular	**Plural**		**Notes**
I You He **worked.** She It	We You **worked.** They		The simple past tense is used to talk about actions or situations in the past. This chapter focuses on regular verbs. These verbs use the *-ed* ending.

B. Pronunciation

The *-ed* ending has three different pronunciations:

- ■ /t/ after voiceless sounds such as /p/ and /k/
- ■ /d/ after voiced sounds such as /v/ and /g/
- ■ /id/ after /t/ and /d/

/t/	/d/	/id/
helped	lived	needed
watched	cleaned	started
worked	hugged	wanted

1 Do you know the meanings of all the verbs in the list below? Underline any you don't know. Discuss them with your teacher. Practice the different sounds of the *-ed* ending. You say one of the verbs, and your partner says the past form of that verb.

/t/		/d/		/id/	
fix	pick	arrive	learn	fold	paint
help	talk	clean	listen	hate	start
kiss	wash	enter	love	invite	visit
like	watch	hug	return	lift	wait
miss	work	join	stay	need	want

2 Use the pictures and cues on page 115 to make sentences. Use the past tense of the verbs.

clean	iron	watch
fix	listen to	wash
fold	✓stay	

Example: *In the 1950s, most women stayed at home.*

at home

1. the clothes

2. the clothes

3. the clothes

4. the house

5. the children

6. the meals

7. their husbands

C. Spelling

Words ending in consonant + *y*		Words ending in vowel + *y*		Notes
study	studied	enjoy	enjoyed	For verbs ending with a consonant + *y*, change *y* to *i* and add *-ed*. Verbs ending with a vowel + *y*, add *-ed* only.
try	tried	play	played	

One vowel + one consonant		One vowel + *w* or *x*		Notes
hug	hugged	fix	fixed	For most verbs ending with one vowel and one consonant, double the final consonant and add *-ed*. For verbs ending with vowel + *w* or *x*, add *-ed* only.
plan	planned	sew	sewed	
shop	shopped			

Common Exceptions				
	enter	entered	open	opened
	happen	happened	travel	traveled
	iron	ironed	visit	visited
	listen	listened		

Note: For verbs ending in *e*, add *-d* only: *arrive → arrived*.

3 Complete each group of sentences with the verbs listed. Use the simple past tense.

1. *kiss, walk, hug*   In the 1950s my grandfather <u>hugged</u> and _____ my grandmother goodbye in the morning. Then he _____ out the door.

2. *wash, walk, stay, dress*   My grandmother _____ home. She _____ the breakfast dishes. Then she _____ the children and _____ the children to school.

3. *wash, iron, fold*   After that she _____ and _____ the clothes. She _____ the shirts.

4. *pick, clean, water*   She _____ the floors. Then she _____ the garden and _____ some roses.

5. *watch, shop, talk*   In the afternoon, she _____ on the telephone to her friend or _____ TV. Sometimes she _____ for food.

6. *talk, walk, travel, work*   My father _____ to the train. He _____ one hour into the city. Then he _____ at his desk all morning. He _____ on the phone a lot.

7. *work, enjoy, wait*   At noon, he _____ a long lunch at a restaurant with co-workers. Then he _____ in the office until 5:00. At 5:30 he _____ for the train to go home.

8. *change, relax, arrive*   At 7:00 he _____ home. He _____ his clothes and _____ with the newspaper.

9. *help, love, listen*   My grandparents _____ dinner time. They _____ to the children's stories. After dinner, they _____ the children with their homework.

D. Negative Statements

Long Form		Contraction	
Subject + *did* + *not* + verb		**Subject + *didn't* + verb**	
I You He She It We You They	**did not work.**	I You He She It We You They	**didn't work.**

4   Read the information about Christine's grandfather on page 117. The sentences that follow are not correct. Correct the sentences as in the examples.

Examples: Robert joined the army.

Robert didn't join the army. He joined the navy.

He was a vice-president.

He wasn't a vice-president. He was a supervisor.

Name: Robert L. Nathanson
Eye Color: blue
Hair Color: brown
Height: 6'2"
Weight: 210 lbs.
Birth Date: February 15, 1913
Branch of Service: Navy
Length of Service: 1941–1950
Rank: General

Job: Supervisor
Awards: 6 for bravery
Area Served In: New York
Hobbies: Plays tennis

1. He worked in California.
2. He served in the military for six years.
3. He received two awards.
4. He was a captain in the navy.
5. He had brown eyes and blue hair.
6. He played soccer.
7. He weighed 180 pounds.
8. He was 5'10".

E. Yes/No Questions and Short Answers

Questions		Short Answers			
Did + subject + verb		**Affirmative**		**Negative**	
Did { I, you, he, she, it, we, you, they } **work?**		Yes, { I, you, he, she, it, we, you, they } **did.**		No, { I, you, he, she, it, we, you, they } **didn't.**	

5   Read the information about Christine's grandmother. One student uses the eight sentences below to make yes/no questions. The other student answers the questions. Then change roles.

Name: Catherine Nathanson
Residence: 2109 Hillside Drive
          Queens, New York
Telephone: 724-0000
Marital Status: Married
Maiden Name: Molina
Children: 2
Eye Color: Brown
Hair Color: Brown
Height: 5'4"
Weight: 110 lbs.

Birth Date: May 28, 1918
Job: Bank Teller
Work Experience: None
Attitude: Works very hard
          enjoys her job

Examples: Catherine lived in New York.
    A.   Did Catherine live in New York?
    B.   Yes, she did.
She was married.
    A.   Was she single?
    B.   No, she wasn't.

1. My grandmother worked in a bank.
2. She had brown hair and brown eyes.
3. She weighed 110 pounds.
4. She had two children.
5. She was born in 1918.
6. She was married.
7. Her telephone number was 724-0000.
8. She liked to read.

F. Subject Questions with Who or What

	Examples	Notes
Statement	My father had an accident.	To ask about a subject, use *who* or *what* + past tense verb. Do not use *did* in these questions.
Question with *who*	***Who* + past tense verb** **Who** had an accident?	
Statement	An accident happened last night.	
Question with *what*	***What* + past tense verb** **What** happened last night?	

G. Information Questions

Statements	I studied English at the library from eight to ten every night. She studied French with her roommate on weekends.
Yes / No Questions and Possible Answers	***Did* + subject + verb** **Did** you **study** every night? Yes, I did. **Did** she **study** every night? Yes, she did.
Information Questions and Possible Answers	**Question word + *did* + subject + verb** **How often did** you **study?** I studied every night. **How long did** you **study?** I studied for two hours. **What did** you **study?** I studied English. **Where did** you **study?** I studied at the library. **When did** she **study?** She studied on weekends. **What did** she **study?** She studied French. **Who* did** she **study** with? She studied with her roommate.

*Note: In formal English, *whom* is used for these questions. In spoken English, *who* is more common.

6   Christine's grandfather was in the military for nine years. Here is some information about Robert's experience in the navy. For each sentence, make questions about the underlined words.

Example: The United States entered the war in 1941.

When did the United States enter the war?

1. My grandfather joined the navy.

2. He was in the navy for nine years.

3. He was a general.

4. He stayed in four different places.

5. He worked in dangerous places.

6. The work was dangerous but important.

7. He enjoyed his work.

8. The navy was terrible.

9.   He hated <u>the navy</u>.

10.   He missed <u>my grandmother</u>.

11.   He wrote to <u>my grandmother</u> almost every night.

12.   <u>The war</u> lasted for four long years.

Using What You've Learned

7   **Playing a Guessing Game.**   Play Twenty Questions. Pretend you are a famous person from the past. Other students have to guess your name. They can ask you questions in the past tense, but you can only answer yes or no.

8   **Telling Stories.**   In small groups, talk about life 50 years ago. What was a typical woman's life like? What was a typical man's life like?

Now talk about life today. What is a woman's life like? What is a man's life like? Are men's and women's roles changing?

After you talk about life, past and present, use your ideas to write a short composition.

PART 3

So, Could, Had to

Setting the Context

Prereading Questions   Did your parents study at the university? How did your mother and your father meet?

Love at First Sight

My parents were graduate students at the university together. My mother wanted to be an architect, so she studied engineering. My father loved the piano, so he majored in music. He had to practice for several hours   5
every day.

My mother's cousin was a student in the music program. She introduced my parents to each other. It was love at first sight. They wanted to spend their lives together, so they   10
couldn't wait for graduation. They got married before they graduated!

Check Your Understanding

1. What did Christine's mother want to be?
2. What did she study?
3. What did Christine's father major in?
4. Was it love at first sight for Christine's parents?
5. Did they graduate before they got married?

A. So

	Examples	Notes
Two Sentences	My parents didn't have much money. They couldn't buy a car.	So means "as a result." So can join two sentences.
One Sentence	My parents didn't have much money, **so** they couldn't buy a car.	A comma is used before so.

1   Omit *because* and use *so* in the following sentences. Add commas and make other necessary changes.

Example: My mother couldn't study at home because she needed quiet.
   My mother needed quiet, so she couldn't study at home.

1. My parents didn't have a lot of money because they were students.
2. Their apartment was small because the rent was cheap.
3. They were happy because they were in love.
4. My father gave performances because he was a musician.
5. My mother studied at night because she had classes all day.
6. My parents had a big celebration because they graduated the same year.
7. My father wanted to work at a university because he wanted to teach music.
8. My mother worked for a small company because she needed to get experience.

2   Match the sentences in Column A with the sentences in Column B. Then join the sentences with *so*. Remember to change the punctuation. The first one is done for you.

Column A	Column B
1. My father needed money when he was a student.	a. She didn't make much money.
2. My mother wanted to be an architect.	b. She began to earn more money.
3. My mother's first job was as an assistant.	c. My mother got pregnant.
4. My parents didn't have a lot of money when they got married.	d. He taught piano to children in the afternoons.
5. Later, my mother started her own business.	e. He was happy.
6. My father got a job at the university.	f. My mother stayed home to take care of me.
7. They wanted to start a family.	g. She needed to understand math and engineering.
8. I was born.	h. They lived in a one-room apartment.

1. *My father needed money when he was a student, so he taught piano to children in the afternoons.*

2. _____

3. _____

4. _____

5. _____

6. _____

7. _____

8. _____

3   Use your imagination and the word *so* to complete the following sentences.

Example: My mother got pregnant, *so she stopped working.*

1. The apartment was too small for three people, _____.

2. My father continued to perform at concerts, _____.

3. My mother worked part-time, _____.

4. Two years later they decided to have another child, _____.

5. It's very hot today, _____.

6. It's late and I'm tired, _____.

7. I'm hungry now, _____.

8. I like learning English, _____.

B. Expressing Past Abilities with Could—Statements and Questions

Affirmative	Negative	Notes
Subject + *could* + verb	**Subject + *couldn't* / *could not* + verb**	
I You He She } **could work.** It We They	I You He She } **couldn't work.** It **could not work.** We They	*Could* and *couldn't* (*could not*) are used to talk about past abilities. The simple form of a verb always follows *could, couldn't,* and other modal auxiliaries.

Yes/No Questions	Possible Answers	
Could + subject + verb	Affirmative	Negative
Could { I you he she it we you they } work?	Yes, { I you he she it we you they } could.	No, { I you he she it we you they } couldn't.

4 Use *could* or *couldn't* (*could not*) to complete these sentences about the United States.

1. In my grandmother's time, women ___couldn't___ work and have a family. They ___could___ stay home with their children.

2. Women _____ be nurses or teachers. They _____ be doctors or lawyers.

3. Men _____ stay home with their children. Women _____ stay home and enjoy their families.

4. Women _____ join the military. They _____ fight.

5. Women _____ drive cars. Women _____ drive buses or trucks.

6. Women _____ vote. A woman _____ hope to become president or vice-president.

C. Expressing Past Needs with Had to

Form	Subject + *had to* + verb		
Singular	**Plural**		**Notes**
I You He She It } **had to** study.	We You They } **had to** study.		*Had to* + verb is used to talk about needs or obligations in the past.

5 Christine's mother developed her career and had children. It wasn't easy! Use *had to* and the cues to make complete sentences. Then, use your imagination to add ideas to the list.

Example: my mother / cook quickly most of the time.
> *My mother had to cook quickly most of the time.*

1. my father / learn to change diapers
2. my parents / clean the house on the weekend
3. the children / help around the house
4. the family / eat simple meals
5. my father / start to cook

6. my mother / find a little time to relax

7. _____

8. _____

Using What You've Learned

6 **Comparing Past and Present Abilities.** Make a list of at least five things women (or men) can do today that they couldn't do in the past. Make sentences with *can* and *couldn't*. Compare your sentences and share your ideas.

Example: drive buses

> *Women can drive buses today, but they couldn't (do that) 20 years ago.*

7 **Comparing Past and Present Situations.** Compare your life in the past to your life today. Use this chart, and try to make a list of five items for each category. Then make complete sentences. Finally, compare your experiences. Begin by telling about your past situation: (Five) years ago, I was (wasn't) . . . Then tell about your present situation: Today I am (not) . . .

Example: *Five years ago, I was in Taiwan. I had to work, so I couldn't go to school everyday.*

Had to do	Could do	Couldn't do	Can do	Can't do
1. *work*		*go to school*		
2.				
3.				
4.				
5.				

PART 4 | Review of Chapters 1 through 5

Setting the Context

Prereading Questions Today, men and women can have almost any job they want. Do women usually do certain kinds of jobs? Are there some jobs that men usually do?

Cops and Robbers

I was the first child, but I wasn't alone for long. In the next four years, my mother had two boys.

It was great having brothers! The three of us were pretty close in age, so we played together all the time. Our favorite game was cops and robbers. It's funny. Everybody always wanted to be a robber. Of course, someone had to be the cop, 5 and it was usually me.

Well, I am an adult now, and I'm married, but I still love cops and robbers. Except there's one big difference. I'm a real police officer, so it's not a game anymore.

Check Your Understanding   Circle T for *True* or F for *False*. Correct the false sentences.

1. T F Christine wasn't the first child.
2. T F She has two brothers and one sister.
3. T F Their favorite game was basketball.
4. T F Christine wanted to be a robber.
5. T F Today she is a police officer.

1   Add the correct form of the verb, and add prepositions where needed.

It's hard to be a police officer, but it's never boring! Just last month there was a mugging* near the police station.

1.   The mugging _happened_ (happen) _on_ a Saturday _in_ the summer.

2.   In fact, it _____ (be) late _____ night _____ July 17, 2000.

3.   Two tourists _____ (be) _____ the sidewalk _____ 11:30 P.M.

4.   They _____ (have) a lot of money _____ their pockets.

5.   Two muggers _____ (be) there _____ the same time.

6.   They _____ (have) guns _____ their hands.

7.   The muggers _____ (rob) the tourists.

8.   The tourists _____ (walk) into the police station _____ midnight.

9.   I talked _____ them for 30 minutes, _____ 12:00 A.M. _____ 12:30 A.M.

10.   _____ the morning, I _____ (be) able to catch the muggers.

11.   Their trial _____ (be) _____ August.

12.   They _____ (be) in prison _____ two _____ four years.

2   Pretend you are a police officer. There was a bank robbery a few minutes ago. You just arrived at the bank. Use the underlined words as cues to make questions from these sentences.

Examples: _I_ saw the robbery.
Who saw the robbery?
I saw everything.
What did you see?

1.   The robbery happened at 10:30 A.M.
2.   A man with long, blond hair walked in the front door.
3.   He was about 20 years old.
4.   He talked to a teller.**

---

*Mugging a robbery that happens to a person on the street.
**Teller a bank employee who works behind a counter.

5. He <u>handed her a note</u>.
6. The note said, "<u>Give me all your money</u>!"
7. He showed her <u>his gun</u>.
8. <u>The teller</u> gave him the money.

3 Correct the prepositions in these sentences. In some cases, more than one preposition may be correct.

under

1. The demonstrators are walking ~~on top of~~ the bridge.
2. The man with a camera is standing above the bridge.
3. The police are far from the demonstration.
4. A demonstrator is under the police car.
5. The police car is in back of the demonstration.
6. The helicopter is flying on top of the demonstration.
7. The horses are far from the man with a camera.
8. A policeman is standing under two horses.
9. The people with the banner are walking over each other.
10. A dog is standing above the man with a camera.

4 Join each pair of sentences on the following page with *because, so,* or *but.*

Example: My brothers are not policemen. They have interesting lives.
My brothers are not policemen, but they have interesting lives.

Robert

1. Robert started college. He couldn't finish.
2. He couldn't finish college. He didn't have enough money.
3. He didn't have enough money. He started looking for a job.
4. Now he makes a lot of money. He doesn't like his job.
5. He doesn't like his job. He has to work a lot.
6. He has to work a lot. He is often very tired.
7. He has to work a lot. There is a lot of work to do.

John

8. John joined the air force. He wanted to fly planes.
9. He joined the air force. He did not become a pilot.
10. His eyes are very bad. He could not learn to fly.
11. He tried new glasses. The glasses didn't help.
12. He wanted to be a pilot. He became a computer operator.
13. He loves his job. He is going to keep his job.
14. He loves his job. He still wants to be a pilot.

5 Use pronouns to complete the dialogues. Use subject pronouns (*I, you, he, she, it, we, they*), object pronouns (*me, you, him, her, it, us, them*) or possessives (*my, your, his, her, our, their*).

1. A. Do you know Christine?

   B. Yes, _____ do. I know _____ very well. _____ is a police officer.

2. A. Did you know John and his wife are getting divorced?

   B. Yes, _____ did. I talked to _____ last week. _____ are both pretty depressed.

3. A. You're married. What does _____ wife do?

   B. _____ wife's a bus driver. What about _____ wife?

4. A. Did you and Robert go to the movie?

   B. No, _____ didn't. Both of _____ were too busy.

5. A. We just bought a new house. _____ house is beautiful!

   B. I'd love to see _____.

6. A. Did Christine catch the mugger?

   B. Yes, _____ did. She caught _____ in July.

7. A. Did you know Christine got a new car?

   B. Yes, _____ 's black and white. You have a new car too, don't _____ ?

   A. Right, but _____ 's purple.

8. A. Are Tony and Ana going to get married?

   B. _____ 'm not sure, but I see _____ together a lot.

9. A. I have two children. _____ children are four and six.

   B. Mike and Susan have two children too.

   A. How old are _____ children?

10.   A. Are you going to find a new job?

B. _____ might. My job now bores _____.

11.   A. Are Robert and John going to finish college?

B. No, _____ aren't. School is difficult for _____.

12.   A. We just bought two new bicycles. _____ new bicycles are red.

B. Mike and Susan also have new bikes, but _____ bikes are blue.

6   Complete this reading in the correct verb tense. Use the past, present, present continuous, and future tenses.

My name _is_ (be) Richard. I _____ (be) Christine's husband. Christine and
        ₁

I _____ (be) introduced in college 23 years ago. She _____ (be) a police
    ₂   ₃

science student. I _____ (be) an engineering student. After a while, we
              ₄

_____ (start) going out on dates. Pretty soon we _____ (be) in love.
    ₅   ₆

Well, I _____ (not finish) college. After two years, I _____ (drop
          ₇   ₈

out*). Christine _____ (not drop out). She _____ (receive) her degree
                  ₉   ₁₀

after four years. We _____ (be) married after she _____ (graduate). In
                        ₁₁   ₁₂

1975, we _____ (move) to Houston, Texas.
          ₁₃

Now we _____ (live) near Houston. Both of us _____ (work). She
            ₁₄   ₁₅

_____ (have) a job with the police department. I _____ (work) for a de-
    ₁₆   ₁₇

partment store. Christine _____ (like) her job more than I like mine. She also
                            ₁₈

_____ (make) more money. I _____ (want) to go back to school. But I
    ₁₉   ₂₀

think I _____ (be) just too old! Next year I _____ (look) for another job.
          ₂₁   ₂₂

7   Complete this reading with *can, must,* or *have to*. In some cases, more than one answer is correct.

When I was a child, I didn't have much freedom. We give our daughter, Marisa, a lot

more freedom than I had. For example, she ___*can*___ go to friends' homes after school.

She _____ go out on dates. She _____ use our car in the day or at night.
        ₁   ₂

_____

Drop out to leave school before finishing.

She also has a lot of responsibilities. For example, she _____ cook dinner
3
twice a week. She _____ do the dishes four times a week. She _____ help clean
4   5
the house. She _____ finish all her homework.
6

Using What You've Learned

8 **Making Rules.**   Imagine that you and your partner are the parents of twins. One of
your twins is a boy; the other is a girl. They are both 17 years old. Give each child a
name and then make a list of rules that each child must follow. List at least ten rules.
Use the following modal verbs: *must, have to, can, can't, should,* and *shouldn't.*

1. _____

2. _____

3. _____

4. _____

5. _____

6. _____

7. _____

8. _____

9. _____

10. _____

9 **Reporting a Robbery.**   Look at the following photo. Imagine that you are a television reporter and you are preparing a story about a robbery that happened yesterday.
Give as many details as possible. Write in the past tense. Practice reading your story.

Read your story to your group. Each group chooses one newscaster to read the story to
the whole class.

10 **Talking About Your Life.**   In Activity 6, Richard talks about his life. Begin by talking to a partner about your life. What did you do in the past? What about now? What are your plans for the future? Finally, write a short essay about your life. Begin by introducing yourself. Then talk about your past, your present, and your future. Try to use the following verb tenses at least once: simple past, simple present, present continuous, and simple future.

_____

_____

_____

_____

_____

_____

_____

_____

_____

_____

_____

_____

_____

_____

_____

_____

_____

_____

_____

_____

_____

_____

_____

_____

_____

_____

_____

Video Activities: Women's Football

Before You Watch.

1. Which of these sports do you like to play or watch?

   a. football   b. soccer   c. basketball   d. tennis

2. Which of the sports above do women usually *not* play?

Watch.

1. What sport do you see?

   a. soccer   b. football   c. basketball

2. Who is playing?

   a. men   b. women   c. both men and women

3. When did Kim Ketchum begin playing?

   a. in high school   b. a year ago   c. last month

4. Why does she play?

   a. wants to make money   b. loves the game   c. father is a coach.

Watch Again.

1. Check the people that you see or hear at the football game.

   _____ cheerleaders   _____ police   _____ fans

   _____ announcers   _____ doctors   _____ a coach

2. Complete the name of Kim's football team. _____ Vixens

   a. Michigan   b. Minnesota   c. Minneapolis   d. Montana

3. Kim's team is part of a football league. What is the abbreviation of its name?

   a. WFL   b. LPFL   c. WPFL

4. How much money has Kim made so far?

   a. $0   b. $100   c. $1,000

After You Watch.   Complete these sentences about professional basketball player, Sheryl Swoopes. Write the correct form of the verb.

1. Sheryl Swoopes _____ (be) born in Texas in 1971.

2. She _____ (play) basketball at Texas Tech University.

3. At Texas Tech, she _____ (score) 1,000 points in 46 games.

4. Then she _____ (start) playing for the U.S. National team after college.

5. In 1996, Sheryl and her teammates _____ (be) Olympic champions.

6. She _____ (join) the Houston Comets in 1997.

Chapter 6

Sleep and Dreams

PART 1	# The Simple Past Tense with Some Irregular Verbs; *Too* and *Either*

Setting the Context

We spend about 30 percent of our lives asleep and during much of that time we dream. No one knows for certain the meaning of our dreams, but scientists who study dreams believe that they hold important messages. In the following passage a woman tells about one of her dreams.

Prereading Questions   Look at the picture. What time of year is it? What is the girl doing?

The Ice Girl

Last night, I had a dream about my childhood. I was very young, and I was in my grandmother's house. The dream began in the autumn, but suddenly it became winter. I was inside my house, but then I went outside. I did some strange things outside. I ate one icicle after another, and they froze my tongue and my mouth. 5
Then my face froze, and after that my arms froze and my legs began to freeze. I almost became an "ice girl." Before I froze completely, my grandmother came outside. She put her arms around me, and just then, spring began. . . . And I became "me" again.

Check Your Understanding   Circle T for *True* or F for *False*. Correct the false sentences.

1. T F The young girl was in her cousin's house.
2. T F The dream began in autumn.
3. T F First, her feet froze.
4. T F Her grandfather put his arms around her.
5. T F She became herself again.

Does this dream have a special meaning? What do you think it is?

A. Irregular Verbs

Simple Form	Past Tense Form	Notes
become	became	Some verbs do not use *-ed* in the past form. These are called irregular verbs. Here are nine irregular verbs. There are many others. For a more complete list, see Appendix 3, page 260.
begin	began	
come	came	
do	did	
eat	ate	
freeze	froze	
go	went	
have	had	
put	put	

1   Underline all of the irregular past tense verbs in the story about the ice girl on page 132.

2   Complete these sentences. Use the simple past tense of the verbs in parentheses. Remember for the negative form to use *didn't* and the simple form of the verb, not the irregular past form.

1.   First my face ___*froze*___ (freeze).

2.   My heart ___*didn't freeze*___ (not freeze).

3.   The weather _____ (begin) to change to a warm spring temperature.

4.   It _____ (not begin) to snow.

5.   The temperature _____ (become) very warm.

6.   I _____ (not become) an ice girl.

7.   After that, I _____ (go) inside the house.

8.   I _____ (not go) outside again for three days.

9.   For many days, I _____ (eat) hot soup.

10.   For years I _____ (not eat) ice cream.

11.   My younger sister _____ (have) a similar dream once.

12.   My brothers _____ (not have) the ice dream.

13.   I remember that my grandmother _____ (do) wonderful things for me when I was a child.

14.   I _____ (put) a picture of my grandmother next to my bed to protect me.

3   Use the past tense to complete these sentences. Then answer the questions in complete sentences.

1.   Johnny's dreams ___*were*___ (be) always the same. He _____ (have) wings like a
1
bird. He _____ (be) in the air all of
2
the time; he _____ (not be) on the
3
ground at all. He _____ (not go)
4
very high above the ground, but he

_____ (go) fast and far. He _____ (not eat) worms and berries. He
5   6

_____ (eat) hamburgers and french fries. He always enjoyed those dreams.
7

a.   Were Johnny's dreams always the same? _Yes, they were._

b.   Was he high in the sky? _____

c.   Did he have fins like a fish or wings like a bird? _____

2.   For a long time my dreams _____ (be) frustrating. Sometimes I _____

1
2

(go) to the post office in my college. I _____ (begin) to turn the lock. I

3

_____ (not do) it right. I could never open it! Other times, I _____ (be)

4
5

at a public telephone. I _____ (become) frustrated because I _____ (not

6
7

have) the correct number. Have you ever had a dream like that?

a.   Were these dreams pleasant? _____

b.   Did he go to the post office in the town? _____

c.   Did he have the correct telephone number, or was it the wrong number?

_____

3.   My math teacher _____ (have) a funny dream. Her dream _____

1
2

(begin) in our Math class. She _____ (come) into the usual room, but the stu-

3

dents _____ (not be) the usual students. All of the students _____ (be)

4
5

famous people. The Backstreet Boys _____ (not have) their homework. Julio

6

Iglesias _____ (eat) a hamburger and fries quickly and then _____

7
8

(begin) to sing the answers to the exercise. What a strange dream!

a.   Did the teacher have a nightmare or a funny dream? _____

b.   Were the students the usual students? _____

c.   What other students came to class? (use your imagination) _____

4.   My English teacher's dream _____ (not be) so funny. It _____ (be)

the first day of class, and it _____ (not begin) well. He _____ (come)

into the room quickly because it _____ (be) so late. The students

_____ (begin) to laugh, so he _____ (look) at himself. He _____

(not have) on his usual professional clothes. He _____ (be) dressed in his

pajamas! Ahhh! The alarm clock. What a relief. It was only a nightmare.

a.   How did the first day of class begin? _____

b.   Why did the students begin to laugh? _____

c.   Did you ever have a similar dream? _____

5. I _____ (have) an amazing dream just last night. In my dream I _____ (go) to work in the morning as usual. But, when I arrived, all my co-workers suddenly _____ (become) very excited. They all _____ (begin) talking to me at once. I _____ (put) up my hands for them to stop, but they just _____ (become) more excited. I _____ (not know) what to do. Finally, it _____ (come) to me. I knew exactly why everyone _____ (be) shouting at me. Unfortunately, when I woke up this morning, I _____ (can't) remember what the problem _____ (be)! Do you have any ideas?

    a.   What kind of dream did I have last night? _____

    b.   How did my co-workers act when I arrived at work? _____

    c.   Give at least three possible reasons why my co-workers were excited.

B. Too *with Short Statements*

Long Form	Short Form	Notes
Marcella had a dream about ice cream, and Mario had a dream about ice cream.	Marcella had a dream about ice cream and Mario **did too.**	When *and* joins two affirmative statements, *too* is sometimes used to make the second statement shorter. The second statement usually has an auxiliary (not a main) verb.
John sees color in his dreams, and Susan sees color in her dreams.	John sees color in his dreams, and Susan **does too.**	
I can answer the question, and you can answer the question.	I can answer the question, and you **can too.**	

C. Using *Either with Short Statements*

Long Form	Short Form	Notes
Marcella didn't eat fish in her dreams, and Mario didn't eat fish in his dreams.	Marcella didn't eat fish in her dreams and Mario **didn't either.**	When *and* joins two negative statements, use *either* instead of *too*. The second statement usually has an auxiliary (not a main) verb.
I'm not tired of grammar, and she isn't tired of grammar.	I'm not tired of grammar, and she **isn't either.**	
They won't be late, and we won't be late.	They won't be late, and we **won't either.**	

4   Sigmund Freud and Carl Jung were psychoanalysts who believed that dreams could explain emotions. Look at the chart on page 136. Then make sentences with *too* and *either.*

Sigmund Freud Sigmund Freud (1856–1939) was the originator of psychoanalysis for the treatment of psychological problems.

Carl Jung Carl Jung (1875–1961) was a Swiss psychiatrist. His theories about using dreams to understand people have influenced many psychiatrists around the world.

	Sigmund Freud	**Carl Jung**
was born in the 1800s	Yes	Yes
lived in Europe	Yes	Yes
studied in the United States	No	No
interpreted dreams	Yes	Yes
worked primarily with children	No	No
had many children	No	No
was a professor at Harvard University	No	No
could speak German	Yes	Yes
had an interest in mental illness	Yes	Yes
studied acupuncture in China	No	No
died in the United States	No	No
is still important in the field of psychiatry	Yes	Yes

1. _____

2. _____

3. _____

4. _____

5. _____

6. _____

7. _____

8. _____

9. _____

10. _____

11. _____

12. _____

In the United States researchers estimate that 3.5 percent of women and 2.5 percent of men receive counseling or psychotherapy. Why do you think there is a higher percentage for women?

5 How many things do the students in your class have in common? For at least five of these questions, find two students who answer yes and two students who answer no. Ask them to write their names in the blanks.

	Yes	No
1. Were you born in the 1970s?		
2. Are you single?		
3. Do you have/want to have more than three children?		
4. Do you speak German?		
5. Did you have coffee this morning?		
6. Can you ski?		
7. Did you study piano when you were a child?		
8. Are you taking a math class?		
9. Did you come to class on time today?		
10. Do you have any brothers?		

Examples: *Elena was born in the 1970s, and Juana was too.*
Hans wasn't born in the 1970s, and Heather wasn't either.

6 Complete this reading. Use the past tense of the verbs in parentheses.

All people dream, so throughout history people have been interested in dreams.

Surely, the cavemen and women _had_ (have) dreams. Perhaps, some of the drawings

they _____ (paint) on the walls of caves _____ (show) dreams and not real-
                1   2

ity. Dreams _____ (have) importance in many ancient cultures. In some cultures,
                3

when special "medicine people" _____ (come) to the home of a sick person, he
                                        4

or she _____ (begin) the treatment by asking about dreams. Some symbols
          5

_____ (be) good "omens" and some _____ (be) bad "omens." People
    6   7

_____ (think) dreams could tell the future, so history sometimes _____
    8   9

(change) because of people's dreams. The Greek philosophers _____ (be) also in-
                                                                  10

terested in dreams. Sigmund Freud _____ (become) famous for his idea that
                                      11

dreams _____ (explain) the past and present psychological state of people. Psy-
            12

chiatrists _____ (begin) to ask people about their dreams. They _____ (do)
              13   14

a great deal of research to understand the importance of dreams. Today, there are many

popular books that help people remember their dreams and understand the symbols.

Using What You've Learned

7   **Talking About Dreams.**

- With a partner, plan the story of a dream and the interpretation of it.
- Then practice a role play of your dream / analysis session. One person is the analyst and the other is the patient.
- Perform your role play for the class.

Example: *Doctor, last night I had a very bizarre dream. I was a microchip in Bill Gates's laptop computer . . .*

8   **Adding Information.**   The whole class sits in a circle. One student makes a statement, and someone else adds another sentence with *either* or *too*. Use the present or the past tense. You don't have to tell the truth. Use your imagination!

Examples: A.   I have five brothers.
          B.   Jake does too.
          C.   I don't have any sisters.
          D.   Eve doesn't either.

PART 2   # The Simple Past Tense—More Irregular Verbs; Tag Questions

Setting the Context

Prereading Questions

- In this section you will read and answer questions about the dreams of several people. We all dream and sometimes our dreams seem rather strange. What do you think the purpose of dreaming is?
- Before you read the following paragraph, look at the picture. Can you explain the dream?

Who Was That Monkey?

A few months ago, Mika had an interesting dream. She was alone in a big forest near the house she grew up in. She found a little monkey. The monkey began to cry. Mika felt sorry for the monkey, but she didn't know what to do.   5
She was very surprised when the monkey spoke, and she understood the language. "My friends left me alone. Then I got lost. I am so sad and afraid." Mika knew what to do. She picked up the monkey and took it home with   10
her. She put the monkey in her bed and brought it hot tea. Then she saw that the monkey wasn't a monkey anymore. The monkey was . . .

Check Your Understanding   Circle T for *True* or F for *False*.

1. T F Mika grew up in a large city.
2. T F She found a family of monkeys.
3. T F The monkey spoke to her and she understood.
4. T F She brought the monkey to the hospital.
5. T F The monkey changed into someone else.

Who do you think the monkey changed into?

1 Read the paragraph about Mika's dream again. Underline all of the verbs in the past tense.

2 Give the past tense forms for the following irregular verbs. (For a complete list of irregular verbs, see Appendix 3, page 260.)

be *was, were* _____   eat _____

become _____   freeze _____

begin _____   go _____

come _____   have _____

do _____   put _____

A. More Irregular Verbs

Simple Form	Past Tense Form
bring	brought
find	found
get	got
grow	grew
grow up	grew up
know	knew
leave	left
speak	spoke
take	took
understand	understood

3 Use the past tense of the verbs in parentheses to complete these sentences.

1. Mika _____ (not grow up) in the United States.

2. She _____ (grow up) in Japan.

3. Mika _____ (have) many strange dreams the first month after she came to the United States.

4. One night, she _____ (find) herself under the sea.

5. She _____ (not find) any other people there.

6. She _____ (not get) scared.

7. In fact, she _____ (get) accustomed to her new surroundings.

8. She _____ (speak) to an orange octopus and a pink sea horse.

9. Unfortunately, they _____ (not speak) Japanese or English.

10. Then she _____ (leave) them to look for someone familiar.

11. But, the octopus _____ (not leave) her side.

12. As a result, she _____ (bring) him with her.

13. She _____ (not bring) the sea horse.

14. Somehow she _____ (know) the octopus was an old friend.

15. She _____ (not know) where to go next.

16. She _____ (take) a turn at a big rock.

17. Then she _____ (understand) the true identity of the octopus.

4 Complete these readings about dreams with past tense forms of the verbs in parentheses. Then answer the questions. Use complete sentences in your answers.

1. Mario __*was*__ (be) alone in a big empty space. Then he _____ (find) something beautiful on the ground. He _____ (pick) it up. It _____ (look)
like a piece of a rainbow. Somehow he _____ (know) what to do. He
_____ (begin) to run. Finally he _____ (find) a rainbow with a piece
missing. It _____ (not have) any color. He _____ (put) the piece in the
rainbow. The rainbow _____ (become) bright and colorful!

a.   Where was Mario? _He was alone in a big empty space._ _____

b.   What did he find? _____

c.   What did he do with it? _____

d.   What did it look like? _____

e.   What did he begin to do? _____

f.   What did he find next? _____

g.   What happened when he put his piece in the rainbow? _____

h.   Do you think this was a good dream or a bad dream? _____

2.   Lee _____ (grow) up in Korea, but in his dream, he _____ (be) a baby
             1   2

in an English-speaking country. Everyone _____ (look) Asian, but they
                                                                      3

_____ (speak) English. He _____ (not be) confused, it _____ (be)
        4   5   6

very natural. His mother _____ (bring) something strange to the table for break-
                                               7

fast. It _____ (be) bright blue! He and his sisters _____ (take) a taste
              8   9

and it _____ (taste) delicious. They _____ (eat) and _____ (smile).
              10   11   12

a.   Where did Lee grow up? _____

b.   In his dream, where was he? _____

c.   What language did everyone speak? _____

d.   Was he confused? _____

e.   What did his mother bring to the table for breakfast? _____

f.   What color was the food? _____

g.   How did it taste? _____

h.   In your opinion, why did Lee have this kind of dream? _____

3.   In Kate's dream, she _____ (want) to take her dog for a walk. She _____
                                            1   2

(bring) a ball for the dog to play with. She _____ (open) the door and they
                                                                       3

_____ (leave) the house. Immediately, they _____ (begin) to fall down, down,
        4   5

down. She _____ (not be) afraid and they _____ (not get) hurt. She _____
                      6   7   8

(get) up and _____ (look) around. They _____ (be) in a new world. Everything
                            9   10

_____ (have) a bright yellow color. She _____ (have) a warm, happy feeling.
        11   12

a.   In her dream, what did Kate want to do? _____

b.   What did she bring for the dog? _____

c.   What happened when they left the house? _____

d.   Was she afraid? _____

e.   Did they get hurt? _____

f.   Where were they? _____

g.   What feeling did she have? _____

h.   In your opinion, does Kate like new experiences or is she afraid of them?

_____

B. Tag Questions

Statement	Statement + Tag Questions	Notes
Mario found something beautiful.	Mario found something beautiful, **didn't he?**	
Kate has a dog.	Kate has a dog, **doesn't she?**	
Lee is Korean.	Lee is Korean, **isn't he?**	Sometimes you think something is true, but you're not sure. To make sure, use tag questions.
In his dream, Lee wasn't in Asia.	In his dream, Lee wasn't in Asia, **was he?**	
Lee's mother really can't speak English.	Lee's mother really can't speak English, **can she?**	
In the dream, she spoke English.	In the dream, she spoke English, **didn't she?**	

 **5**   Prepare some questions to interview a classmate. Make the following sentences into tag questions. Then ask your partner the first eight questions. Your partner can ask you the next eight questions.

1.   You did the homework last night, _*didn't you?*_

2.   You like your English class, _____?

3.   Your mother doesn't speak English, _____?

4.   You were born in the last century, _____?

5.   You can speak a lot of English now, _____?

6.   Elvis Presley was a famous rock singer, _____?

7.   Soccer is a popular sport in many countries, _____?

8.   Pele was one of the greatest soccer players, _____?

9.   This is a good grammar book, _____?

10.   You can make tag questions now, _____?

11.   Our teacher is very nice, _____?

12.   You had an interesting dream, _____?

13.   We finished Chapter 5, _____?

14.   The Beatles were a popular English group, _____?

15.   Jazz music originally came from the United States, _____?

16.   Yoga is a form of exercise from India, _____?

6   Work with a new partner. Add tag questions to the following statements and then ask your partner the questions. One person asks the first six questions and the other person asks the next six questions.

1.   Today isn't Sunday, _is it?_

2.   You weren't born in an English-speaking country, _____?

3.   You didn't learn English as your first language, _____?

4.   You can't compete in the Olympics, _____?

5.   Our teacher doesn't give a lot of homework, _____?

6.   We don't always remember dreams, _____?

7.   You can't speak five languages, _____?

8.   You didn't have a nightmare last night, _____?

9.   You don't have 12 children, _____?

10.   You aren't a famous movie star, _____?

11.   Yesterday wasn't a holiday, _____?

12.   English isn't so difficult, _____?

Using What You've Learned

7   **Asking Your Partner.**   Work with a partner. Ask your partner questions about his or her life. Ask at least six tag questions. Make three positive and three negative questions. Then change roles.

Examples: _You are married, aren't you?_
You didn't grow up in Switzerland, did you?

8   **Telling Stories.**   Look at the chart that tells one interpretation of the symbolic meaning of animals in dreams. With your classmates, add some more animals and possible meanings. Be creative!

Animal	Symbolic Meaning
birds	freedom
dogs	loyalty and love
lion	strength
monkey	?

- Invent a dream or write about a real dream that you had with an animal or some animals in it. Write one paragraph starting with *Last night I had a dream . . .*
- Exchange your paragraph with one person in the group. Use the chart about symbolic meaning to write a paragraph to explain the dream. Be creative!
- Read your dream paragraph and the interpretation paragraph to your group. Listen to the other paragraphs. Choose the most creative to read to the class.

Symbols and images in dreams change with each passing decade. Now people have elevators, computers, shopping malls, and parking lots in their dreams. Our great grandparents didn't have some of these symbols. Can you think of other symbols that are recent?

PART 3

The Simple Past Tense—More Irregular Verbs; *Even though; Used to*

Setting the Context

Prereading Questions Look at the picture below. Why do you think the students look so tired?

Teenagers Need More Sleep!

When you were an infant, you used to sleep 17 or 18 hours a day. By the time you turned five, you spent ten or 12 hours a day asleep. You probably still took a nap in the afternoon. As a young adult, your body needed about eight to nine hours of sleep a night. Even though adults need eight hours of sleep a night, many people do not sleep more than six hours. They miss valuable sleep time.

5

Teenagers don't get enough sleep, either. Researchers have studied teenage sleep patterns. They discovered that because of their body chemistry, many teenagers could not go to sleep early. Even though they went to bed late, they had to get up early for school. Researchers found that only 15 percent of teenagers got enough sleep during the school week. In one study, a school changed the   10 starting time from 8:00 A.M. to 9:30 A.M. After that, grades improved.

Check Your Understanding   Circle T for *True* or F for *False*. Correct the false sentences.

1.   T   F   When you were an infant, you used to sleep ten hours a night.
2.   T   F   At the age of five, you probably took a nap every afternoon.
3.   T   F   Teenagers need only six hours of sleep a night.
4.   T   F   Researchers discovered that teenagers could not go to sleep late.
5.   T   F   Even though teenagers went to bed late, they had to get up early.
6.   T   F   When one school changed the starting time, grades improved.

How many hours of sleep did you get last night?
What time did you go to bed?
What time did you get up?

1   Fill in the past tense forms of these irregular verbs. If you can't remember, see page 140.

bring _____	know _____
find _____	leave _____
get _____	speak _____
grow _____	take _____
grow up _____	understand _____

A. Even though

But	Even Though	Notes
Adults need eight hours of sleep a night, **but** many only sleep six hours. They went to bed late, **but** they had to get up early.	**Even though** adults need eight hours of sleep a night, many only sleep six hours. **Even though** they went to bed late, they had to get up early.	In many sentences, *even though* can be used instead of *but*. *Even though* can come at the beginning of these sentences. *But* comes in the middle.

2   Rewrite the following sentences. Omit *but* and use *even though*.

Example: Many people should go to bed before 10:00, but they go to bed later.
    Even though many people should go to bed before 10:00, they go to bed later.

1.   Parents tell teenagers to go to bed early, but teenagers often stay up late.
2.   Teenagers need more sleep, but most schools begin early in the morning.

3. Most people feel sleepy after lunch, but important classes are often scheduled in the early afternoon.

4. It's important to go to bed early before an exam, but many students stay up late studying.

5. Last night Susan went to bed at midnight, but she had to get up at 6:00 A.M.

6. Susan didn't go to bed until 2:00 A.M. on Saturday night, but she could sleep until noon on Sunday.

7. Joe was asleep in chemistry class, but his teacher didn't notice.

8. Joe tried to go to bed early, but he couldn't fall asleep until after midnight.

3   Match the sentences in the following list. Then, make sentences with *even though*.

Example: *Even though Mike went to bed at midnight, he had to wake up at 6:30 A.M.*

1. Mike went to bed at midnight.
2. Mike's alarm went off at 6:30.
3. Mike was at the bus station on time.
4. Mike was tired all day.
5. Marie went to bed at 10:00 P.M.
6. Marie had wonderful dreams.
7. Marie drank coffee after dinner.
8. Marie's apartment is noisy.

a. She had no problem sleeping.
b. She didn't have to wake up until 10:00 A.M.
c. Noise doesn't bother her.
d. She couldn't remember them.
e. He had to wake up at 6:30 A.M.
f. He didn't have time for a nap.
g. He didn't hear the alarm until 7:00.
h. The bus was late.

4   Use your imagination to complete the following sentences.

Example: Even though I need eight hours of sleep, *I only get six hours a night.*

1. Even though I go to bed late on the weekends, _____.

2. Even though some people drink coffee in the morning, _____.

3. Even though we have no school on Sunday, _____.

4. Even though I do my homework every night, _____.

5. Even though English is difficult, _____.

6. Even though my teacher explains clearly, _____.

7. Even though we study every day, _____.

8. Even though I don't understand everything, _____.

B. Used to

Examples	Meanings	Notes
You **used to sleep** 17 to 18 hours a day. You **used to wear** diapers when you were a baby.	(You don't sleep 17 to 18 hours a day now.) (You don't wear diapers now.)	*Used to* is followed by a simple verb. It means that something was true in the past but isn't true anymore.

5 Your life is different now from when you were a baby. Read each statement below about when Charlie was a baby. Then tell what is true for Charlie now.

Example: Charlie used to sleep 15 hours a day.
Now he sleeps only six hours a night.

1. Charlie used to crawl on the floor.
2. Charlie used to eat with his fingers.
3. Charlie used to cry when he was hungry.
4. Charlie used to drink milk from a bottle.
5. Charlie used to sit in a high chair.
6. Charlie used to sleep in a crib.
7. Charlie used to play with toys all day.
8. Charlie used to sleep with a teddy bear.

6 Do you remember what your life was like when you were in kindergarten? Make a list of eight things you used to do, but you can't do or don't do anymore.

Example: *I used to play with dolls. I don't do that anymore.*

7 Think about when you were 13 years old. Sit in a circle. Tell one thing you *used to* do when you were 13 years old. Explain if you still do this or if you don't do it anymore.

C. More Irregular Verbs

Simple Form	Past Tense Form	Notes
buy	bought	These sentences have the same meaning:
cost	cost	I bought a computer for $1,500.
pay	paid	The computer cost $1,500.
spend	spent	I paid $1,500 for a computer.
		I spent $1,500 on a computer.

8   Complete these conversations. Use the past forms of the verbs *buy, cost, pay,* and *spend.* Add other information as needed.

1.   *Charlie:* I just __*bought*__ a new __*CD!*__

    Marie: How much did it __*cost?*__

    Charlie: It __*cost $19.99.*__

2.   *Ellen:* I just bought a new _____!
    ₁

    Simon: How much did you _____?
    ₂

    Ellen: I _____.
    ₃

3.   *Monica:* John just ___ a new ___!
    ₁   ₂

    Kate: How much did he _____?
    ₃

    Monica: He _____.
    ₄

4.   *Alfonso:* Martin just ___ a new ___!
    ₁   ₂

    Patty: How much did it _____?
    ₃

    Alfonso: It _____.
    ₄

9   Complete this conversation between Susan and John. Uses the present or past tense of the verbs in parentheses.

Susan: Hey, John! Guess what? I just __*bought*__ (buy) a new tennis racket.

John: Wow! _____ (be) it expensive? How much _____ it _____ (cost)?
    ₁   ₂   ₃

Susan: It _____ (be) a great deal! It only _____ (cost) $150.
    ₄   ₅

John: $150! That _____ (be) a lot of money. You _____ (not buy) anything
    ₆   ₇

else, _____ (do) you?
    ₈

Susan: Well, I _____ (get) a new camera yesterday.
    ₉

John: But, you already _____ (have) a camera. You _____ (buy) it last month.
    ₁₀   ₁₁

You _____ (pay) $350 for it.
    ₁₂

Susan: Yes, but I really _____ (need) a new one now. This new camera _____
                         13   14
(do) many things.

John: How much _____ you _____ (spend) on it?
                          15   16

Susan: I _____ (get) a great deal. This camera usually _____ (cost) $600, but
                 17   18
yesterday it _____ (be) on sale. I only _____ (pay) $450.
                   19   20

John: _____ (be) you crazy? You _____ (have to) pay rent for your apartment
              21   22
tomorrow. Where are you going to get enough money for rent?

Susan: I _____ (not be) sure, but . . . John, _____ you _____ (want) to buy
                 23   24   25
my old camera?

Using What You've Learned

10 **Making Conversations.**   Write at least six short conversations. (Look at the conversations in Activities 8 and 9 for help.) Try to use the verbs *buy, pay, cost,* and *spend* as well as other irregular verbs. Choose two of the conversations and, with your partner, perform them for the class.

PART 4 # The Simple Past Tense—More Irregular Verbs; Reported Speech

Setting the Context

Prereading Questions   Why do people snore? Do you snore? Does someone in your family snore?

Snoring

My older brother Sam had a big problem—he snored. He always said that he didn't snore, but he never heard himself! We used to make jokes about it, but it really wasn't funny. We didn't know it was a serious problem.   5

When Sam got married, his snoring became a bigger problem. His wife didn't think it was funny at all. She thought he had a serious sleep disorder, *apnea.* She wanted him to see a doctor. She knew it could be dangerous, so she made an appointment   10
for him with a sleep specialist. The doctor said that Sam had sleep apnea and needed help.

Check Your Understanding   Circle T for *True* or F for *False*. Correct the false sentences.

1. T F Sam had a serious problem. He walked in his sleep.
2. T F Sam's sisters and brothers used to make jokes about his problem.
3. T F Sam's wife thought it was funny.
4. T F His wife wanted him to see a dentist.
5. T F The doctor said that Sam had insomnia.

1   Give the past tense forms of these irregular verbs. If you can't remember, check pages 132, 140, and 148.

be _____	go _____
become _____	grow up _____
begin _____	have _____
bring _____	have to _____
buy _____	know _____
come _____	leave _____
cost _____	pay _____
do _____	put _____
eat _____	speak _____
find _____	spend _____
freeze _____	take _____
get _____	understand _____

A. More Irregular Verbs

Simple Form	Past Tense Form
hear	heard
know	knew
say	said
think	thought

2   Complete these sentences. Use the past forms of the verbs in parentheses.

1. I _____ (hear) that many people had sleep problems.
2. I _____ (not hear) that doctors had all of the answers.
3. Sam _____ (not know) that he snored.
4. His wife _____ (know) that he had a serious problem.
5. His wife _____ (say), "You need to see a doctor."
6. The doctor _____ (not say) his problem was funny.

7. We _____ (not think) his problem was serious.

8. The doctor _____ (think) Sam had sleep apnea.

B. Reported Speech

When we talk about what someone else said, we often use the verbs *hear, know,* and *say.* This is called reported speech.

Statement	Reported Speech	Notes
"You snore every night." "Your snoring is a serious problem."	His wife said that he snored every night. The doctor said that his snoring was a serious problem.	If the first verb is in the past, the second verb is usually in the past also.

3 Change the statements into reported speech.

1. "Sleep apnea is dangerous."

   Sam's wife heard that _____

2. "People with short, thick necks often have this problem."

   After reading an article, she knew that _____

3. "It isn't easy to live with someone who snores."

   We always said that _____

4. "Many women have the same problem."

   The doctor said that _____

5. "There are solutions to this problem."

   Sam knew _____

6. "Some people stop breathing in their sleep."

   Sam heard that _____

7. "Sam needs help."

   The doctor said that _____

8. "There are several things to change."

   Sam heard that _____

4 Imagine that at the end of each English class there is a wild party. Be creative and make a list of all of the details about the party. Then change them to reported speech. Use *I heard that, I thought that,* or *people said that.*

Example: *Our English teacher always cooks all of the food.*
I heard that our English teacher always cooked all of the food.

1. Our grammar teacher said

   that . . . _____

2. I thought that all of the

   students . . . _____

3.   I heard that the police . . . _____

4.   _____

5.   _____

6.   _____

7.   _____

C. More Irregular Verbs

Simple Form	Past Tense Form
give	gave
lend	lent
see	saw

5   Joan is going to take a long airplane flight, but she is afraid to travel. She wants to be sure to sleep on the plane. Complete the sentences with the past tense forms of the verbs in parentheses.

1.   Her sister _____ (give) her a book called *The Joy of Flying!*

2.   She _____ (not give) her a book about airplane crashes.

3.   Her friend _____ (not lend) her earplugs.

4.   Her friend _____ (lend) her a sleep mask.

5.   On TV Joan _____ (see) a commercial for a special travel store.

6.   She _____ (not see) a commercial for pet food.

7.   She _____ (make) a long list of all of the reasons to enjoy flying.

8.   She _____ (not make) a list of the reasons to avoid flying.

6   Complete the readings with the past tense forms of the verbs in parentheses.

1.   My grandmother always ___*said*___ (say), "I _____ (never have) a good
                                                          1
night's sleep after I _____ (marry) your grandfather." The reason _____
                         2   3
(be) that my grandfather snored. "For months I _____ (put) a pillow over my head
                                                   4
when I _____ (go) to bed. That _____ (be) not a good solution, and it
          5   6
_____ (not work)." Next she _____ (buy) earplugs, but she _____
     7   8   9
(not like) to sleep with them. She _____ (hear) about an herbal tea, so she
                                      10
_____ (make) it for my grandfather every night for a month. Unfortunately, that
     11

_____ (not help) either. At that time, doctors _____ (not think) that snoring
       12   13

_____ (be) a problem. Too bad for Grandpa! Too bad for Grandma!
       14

2. When Marcella _____ (come) to the United States, she _____
                              1   2

(have) a big problem: sleeping. Many people _____ (give) her advice. One per-
                                                              3

son _____ (say), "Take a long, hot bath before you go to bed." Marcella also
        4

_____ (hear) that a good book, herbal teas, warm milk, and soft music
       5

_____ (be) all good ideas. But she still _____ (not sleep) more than five
       6   7

hours a night. In a health food store, she _____ (see) many natural remedies, but
                                                              8

she _____ (be) afraid to take them. She _____ (not want) to take sleeping
        9   10

pills either. She _____ (not know) what else to do, but her mother _____
                        11   12

(know) exactly what to do. She _____ (make) a tape of the songs she sang to
                                        13

Marcella every night when she _____ (be) a baby. After that every night
                                        14

Marcella _____ (go) to sleep easily and she slept like a baby!
              15

Using What You've Learned

7   **Writing a Story.**   Finish the following story. Use the verbs in this chapter and others.
Write at least three more sentences.

   My brother Jim had a big problem. He couldn't get up in the morning.

Read your stories in your group. Choose one story to read to the whole class.

Checking Your Progress

Check your progress with structures from Chapters 5 and 6. Be sure to review any
problem areas.

Part 1.   Choose the correct word(s) to complete each sentence.

1. I didn't finish, and she _____.
    a. did too
    b. didn't either
    c. didn't too
    d. either
    e. neither

2. Tony came late today, _____?
    a. doesn't he
    b. did he
    c. came he
    d. didn't he
    e. wasn't he

3. Even though Jin has a car, _____.
   a. he studies English at school
   b. he takes the bus to school
   c. he does drive to school
   d. he goes to school
   e. he drives to school

4. Who _____ in that bed?
   a. used to sleep
   b. was sleeped
   c. used to sleeping
   d. sleeping
   e. did sleep

5. Juan heard that snoring _____ dangerous.
   a. were
   b. has
   c. will be
   d. is
   e. was

6. Jack's new car _____ a small fortune.
   a. bought
   b. cost
   c. spent
   d. made
   e. paid

7. The doctor _____ about dreams.
   a. didn't spoke
   b. speak
   c. spoke
   d. did spoke
   e. speaked

8. I _____ $2,000 on the computer.
   a. cost
   b. bought
   c. payed
   d. spend
   e. spent

9. My father _____ me $5,000.
   a. gaves
   b. gave
   c. gived
   d. didn't gived
   e. will gives

10. I _____ that you were coming.
   a. heard
   b. hearing
   c. was heard
   d. hears
   e. heared

Part 2. Circle the correct words to complete this story.

Yuka (have / had) a difficult decision to make. Should she (go / goes) to the United
        1   2
States to study English, or should she (staying / stay) in her country? Finally she
                                          3
decided to (go / went). She (hears / heard) that she could (lives / live) with a host family
        4   5   6
and practice English all the time.

    At the airport, she (said / sayed) goodbye to her family and (gets / got) on the
                            7   8
airplane. Soon she (arriving / arrived) in Los Angeles. At first she (didn't saw / didn't see)
                        9   10
her host family. Then she (found / founded) them. But she didn't understand them, and
                              11
they didn't understand her (too / either). Why? Because they (was / were) birds! She
                              12   13
looked around the airport. She (sees / saw) only birds and animals. She
                                      14
(begins / began) to cry. Then her alarm clock went off. Whew! It was only a dream.
    15

Video Activities: Children and Sleep

Before You Watch.

1. How long do most people need to sleep every night?

    a. 6 hours   b. 8 hours   c. 10 hours   d. 12 hours

2. What does our "internal clock" tell us?

    a. when to eat
    b. the time of day
    c. when to sleep and wake up

Watch.

1. How long do young children need to sleep every night?

    a. 6 hours   b. 8 hours   c. 10 hours   d. 12 hours

2. What happens to children who are "sleep-deprived" (who don't get enough sleep)? Check all that apply.

    _____ They don't want to get up in the morning.

    _____ They work harder.

    _____ They can't concentrate very well.

    _____ They get into trouble at school.

Watch Again.

1. Check the things that make children stay up later according to the video.

    _____ homework   _____ television   _____ internal clock

    _____ computers   _____ lights   _____ parents

2. How quickly can you change a child's internal clock?

    a. one hour a week
    b. two hours a day
    c. one hour a day
    d. three hours a week

After You Watch.
Combine the following sentences with *too, either,* or *even though.*

1. My daughter didn't sleep well last night. My son didn't sleep well last night.
2. They went to bed early. They couldn't fall asleep.
3. I read them a story. My husband read them a story.
4. My daughter wasn't tired. My son wasn't tired.
5. This morning my daughter didn't want to get up. This morning my son didn't want to get up.
6. They had school. I let them sleep late.

Chapter 7

Work and Lifestyles

PART 1

The Past Continuous Tense— Affirmative Statements; Contrast of Past and Present Continuous Tenses

Setting the Context

Prereading Questions   What was the man in the picture doing five years ago? What is he doing now? Make a guess.

Then and Now

Five years ago, Andre Cardoso was living in an apartment with his aunt and uncle in Chicago, Illinois. His parents were sending him money. He was studying English and taking computer classes. He liked his English classes, but he loved his computer classes. He was learning as much as possible as fast as possible. At the same time he was   5 meeting new people and making new friends. Life was great!

  After just one year, Andre got a job with a small company in Chicago. He was very good at his job. Eight months later, he got a better job. In the next three years, Andre changed jobs four more times! Now Andre is living in his own apartment in San Francisco, California.   10 He is still working with computers. In fact, he has his own company— Cardoso Consulting. He is very busy, but very happy. He is making a lot of money and he loves his work. Life looks beautiful for him.

Check Your Understanding

1.   Where was Andre living five years ago?
2.   What was he studying?
3.   How many jobs did Andre have in three years?
4.   Where is he living now?
5.   Is he working with computers now?

In the past, many people had one job for life. Today, it is common for people to change jobs several times. How many jobs have you had?

A. Affirmative Statements

Form	Subject + *was or were* + verb + *-ing*		
Singular	**Plural**		**Notes**
I **was working.** You **were working.** He She } **was working.** It	We You } **were working.** They		Use the past continuous tense to talk about past activities in progress at specific times such as *a minute ago, yesterday, last week, last month,* or *last year.*

1 Underline all the past continuous verbs in the reading on page 158.

2 Change the present continuous tense to the past continuous tense in these sentences. Change *now* to *five years ago*.

Example: Andre is working with computers now.
Andre was working with computers five years ago.

1. Andre is living in an apartment now.
2. Andre is making a lot of friends now.
3. He's dating a lot now.
4. He's speaking English all of the time now.
5. He's having a lot of success now.
6. Now he's learning new ways of doing things.
7. He's spending hours and hours working on his computer now.
8. Now he's thinking about his future.

3 Change the following sentences to the past continuous tense. Add one of the time expressions to each sentence. Use each time expression at least once.

Example: Andre is working with computers now.
Andre was working with computers five years ago.

TIME EXPRESSIONS			
five years ago	yesterday	last week	last year

1. Andre is making new friends.
2. Andre is dating a young woman from Spain now.
3. Andre is enjoying life in the United States.
4. People are using computers for everything.
5. We're studying a lot of grammar now.
6. Our class is studying Chapter 5 now.
7. We're speaking English now.
8. I'm living in _____ (your city) now.

4 Meet Andre's neighbors. Complete these sentences. Use the past continuous tense of the verbs in parentheses.

1. My name is Sam. I used to be a plumber, but last year I lost my job. I *was living*

(live) in Pittsburgh, and I _____ (work) at Pittsburgh Plumbing. I
₁

_____ (plan) to work until my retirement. Now I'm living in
₂

Miami, and I'm working for my cousin's company.

2. Hi. I'm Ana. I used to be a teacher, but I wanted to be an actress. Last year I

_____ (live) in Hollywood. I _____ (try) to get a
  ₁

job in the movies. I _____ (dream) about my first movie. Now

I'm a waitress. But you know what? I like it!

3. Hello. My name is Fred. I always wanted my son to go to college, and he did go.

After college, my son _____ (work) with computers, and he

_____ (invent) lots of crazy things. Big companies

_____ (call) him. They _____ (try) to buy some

of his inventions. I _____ (take) the phone messages. Now he's

working in a car wash. What happened?

5 Use your own words and ideas to complete these sentences. Write about yourself.

Example: Last year at this time, I _was working in a bank._

1. A minute ago, I _____.

2. At 6:00 last night, I _____.

3. At midnight last night, I _____.

4. At this time yesterday, I _____.

5. At this time last Saturday, I _____.

6. At this time last week, I _____.

7. At this time last month, I _____.

8. At this time ten years ago, I _____.

B. Contrast of Past and Present Continuous Tenses

	Examples	**Notes**
Present Continuous Tense	We**'re studying** Chapter 7 now. He**'s living** in San Francisco now.	Use the present continuous tense for action happening now.
Past Continuous Tense	We **were studying** Chapter 6 last week. He **was living** in Chicago five years ago.	Use the past continuous tense for action in progress in the past.

6 Meet some of the business people in Andre's neighborhood. Complete these readings. Use the past continuous or present continuous tense of the verbs in parentheses.

1. Last year at this time, I _was looking_ (look) for a job. I _____ (read) the want ads in the newspaper, and I _____ (send) resumes everywhere. I _____ (live / also) on very little money! Finally, I got a job. Today I _____ (work) at Software Systems. I _____ (write) computer programs, and I _____ (help) with some special projects. I'm very happy, and I'm not poor anymore.

2. A year ago, we _____ (look) for jobs. We _____ (apply) for positions everywhere. We _____ (feel) very worried. Then we started our own business. Today we _____ (run) our own design company. We _____ (do) advertising for many small businesses here. We _____ (think) about some new projects too. And we _____ (talk) about hiring an assistant! We feel very lucky today.

Using What You've Learned

7 **Talking About Past Activities.** Tell what you were doing at the times in this chart. Ask other students what they were doing. Write their answers in the chart.

Name	Last night at midnight	Last year at this time	Last Saturday night	After class yesterday
Example: Joe	He was doing homework.	He was living with his family.	He was dancing.	He was studying in the library.

8   **Describing Yourself.**   Write a paragraph about yourself like the ones in Activity 6 on page 161. Use this incomplete paragraph as a model.

Last year at this time, I _____

_____ .

I _____ .

Then _____ .

_____

_____ .

Today I _____

_____ .

PART 2

The Past Continuous Tense— Negative Statements; Questions

Setting the Context

Prereading Questions   Who are the people in the picture? What are they doing?

Success!

A San Francisco independent newspaper is writing a series of articles about successful immigrants. A journalist is interviewing Andre for a short article.

Journalist: When you first came here, you were studying English, right? You were also working at a small computer company, weren't you?

Andre: I was studying English and taking computer classes during the day. I wasn't   5
working at a computer company then. I was working in my uncle's nightclub six nights a week.

Journalist: That's a very heavy schedule. When did you sleep?

Andre: That was the problem. I was learning a lot, and I was making good money, but I wasn't sleeping enough. After about nine months, I was ready to make a 10 change.
Journalist: How did you do that?
Andre: One of my computer science professors hired me as an assistant. I was working about 15 hours a week for her. I wasn't earning as much, but I was sleeping and studying more. I was learning a lot from her too. 15
Journalist: When did you decide to start your own business?
Andre: That was later. I wasn't even dreaming of my own business then. I needed to work for someone else and get some experience first.

Check Your Understanding   Circle T for *True* or F for *False.* Correct the false sentences.

1.   T F Andre was working in a relative's restaurant.
2.   T F He wasn't sleeping enough.
3.   T F A professor hired Andre to work as a singer in a nightclub.

A. Negative Statements

Form	Subject + *was* or *were* + not + *ing*	
Long Form		**Contractions**
I **was not working.**		I **wasn't working.**
You **were not working.**		You **weren't working.**
He		He
She **was not working.**		She **wasn't working.**
It		It
We		We
You **were not working.**		You **weren't working.**
They		They

1   Change these statements to negative sentences. Use contractions.

Example: Andre was working in a restaurant then.
　　　　Andre wasn't working in a restaurant then.

1.   Andre was studying Spanish.
2.   Andre was living in his own apartment in Chicago.
3.   He was singing in a nightclub.
4.   He was spending a lot of money.
5.   I was dancing in a nightclub in Chicago last night.
6.   We were studying Chapter 9 last week.
7.   We were speaking Chinese in class yesterday.
8.   Our teacher was sleeping in class yesterday.

2 Carolina is Andre's sister. Complete her story with the past continuous tense of the verbs in parentheses.

Hi. I'm Carolina, Andre's younger sister. While Andre ___was studying___ (study) in Chicago, I _____ (study) hotel management in New York. I _____ (not live) in the dormitory. I _____ (stay) with my cousins in Connecticut. I _____ (not work) because I _____ (spend) two hours a day on the train. My cousins _____ (not speak) any English to me, and I _____ (not learn) very fast. I _____ (not feel) happy or successful. I _____ (get) a little depressed and frustrated. I didn't know what to do to change my situation.

B. Yes / No Questions and Short Answers

Yes/No Questions	Short Answers	
	Affirmative	**Negative**
Was I **working?**	Yes, you **were.**	No, you **weren't.**
Were you **working?**	Yes, I **was.**	No, I **wasn't.**
Was { he / she / it } **working?**	Yes, { he / she / it } **was.**	No, { he / she / it } **wasn't.**
Were { you / we / they } **working?**	Yes, { you / we / they } **were.**	No, { you / we / they } **weren't.**

3 Write the questions for these statements.

1. ___Were you living here last month?___
   Yes, I was living here last month.

2. _____
   No, Carolina wasn't living in the dormitory.

3. _____
   No, Carolina wasn't working.

4. _____

Yes, Carolina was spending a lot of time on the train.

5. _____

No, her cousins weren't speaking English with her.

6. _____

Yes, I was studying hard last night.

7. _____

No, I wasn't speaking my native language in English class!

8. _____

No, our teacher wasn't speaking to us in Russian.

4 Answer these questions. Write short answers.

Example: Were you visiting Las Vegas last week?
No, I wasn't.

1. Were your classmates working last night?

_____

2. Was your teacher working hard last week?

_____

3. Were you living in Vancouver last year?

_____

4. Were you going to school before you came here?

_____

5. Were you learning a lot in your last job?

_____

6. Were you sleeping at midnight last night?

_____

7. Were we studying Chapter 9 last week?

_____

8. Was it raining last night?

_____

C. Information Questions

Form	Question word + _was/were_ + subject + verb + _ing_ + time expression	
Questions		**Possible Answers**
What was he **doing** yesterday?		He was working.
Where were we **meeting** last year?		We were meeting in San Francisco.
When was it **arriving?**		It was arriving at 3:00.
Why were you **taking** a course last month?		Because I wanted to.
How was she **doing?**		She was doing well.
How much was he **earning?**		He was earning a lot of money.

Form	Who + *was* + verb + *-ing*	
Questions	**Possible Answers**	
Who was doing that job?	John was doing it.	
Who was calling all last night?	David was.	

5   Use these question words to complete the sentences below. More than one word can be used in some sentences.

Who   What   When   Where   Why   How   How much

1. _____ were you doing at 10:00 last night?

2. _____ were you saying a minute ago?

3. _____ was helping you with the assignment?

4. _____ was he going?

5. _____ were you getting to work?

6. _____ were you working there?

7. _____ were they earning money?

8. _____ was he running out the door?

9. _____ was coming in the door?

10. _____ were you earning last year?

Using What You've Learned

6   **Learning About Another Student.**   Write ten true or false statements about things you were doing in the past. The sentences can be affirmative or negative.

1. _____

2. _____

3. _____

4. _____

5. _____

6. _____

7. _____

8. _____

9. _____

10. _____

Now take turns reading your statements to your partner. Decide which of your partner's sentences are true and which are false. Your partner will do the same for your sentences. Finally, tell each other the truth.

Example: A.   Last summer I was working.
           B.   False. I think you were visiting your grandparents.
           A.   You're right. I was visiting my grandparents.

7 **Information Gap.**   Here is more information about Andre and Carolina.

■   One partner is Student A. Look only at the chart labeled Student A.

■   The other partner is Student B. Look only at the cart labeled Student B.

■   Ask information questions to complete your chart.

Student A

Name	10 years ago/living	Last year/dating	Last year/earning	Now earning
Andre	_____	Mina	_____	$200,000 a year
Carolina	Brazil	_____	$2,000 a month	_____

Student B

Name	10 years ago/living	Last year/dating	Last year/earning	Now earning
Andre	Brazil	_____	$40,000 a year	_____
Carolina	_____	nobody	_____	nothing

8 **Writing a Newsletter Article.**   Interview a partner.

■   Write ten interview questions to ask your partner. Use the past continuous tense.

■   Then ask your partner the questions. Take notes on your partner's answers.

Questions	Notes
Example: *Where were you living five years ago?*	*In Argentina.*
1.	
2.	
3.	
4.	
5.	
6.	
7.	
8.	
9.	
10.	

■   Write a newsletter article about your partner. Use your interview notes.

| PART 3 | *While;* Contrast of Simple Past and Past Continuous Tenses |

Setting the Context

Prereading Questions   Look at the picture. Who is the woman? What is she doing?

Making Changes

While Andre was becoming successful in San Francisco, Carolina was having a difficult time in New York. She wasn't learning English fast enough. She wasn't making friends and she wasn't earning any money. She decided to move into the dormitory   5
at her college. Her roommate, Sylvie, was from Toronto, Canada. Sylvie was working in a restaurant. She helped Carolina get a job there. Carolina was so happy. She was speaking English all the time. She was also earning money and meeting people.   10

While she was working, she met the other waiters, waitresses, and chefs. She was learning a lot about the restaurant business, too. One night, when she went to the kitchen for an order, the chef smiled at her. Then he asked her out on a date. They went   15
out dancing after work. While they were dancing, Carolina was thinking about the changes in her life.

Check Your Understanding

1. At first, was Carolina successful in New York?
2. Where was her new roommate working?
3. Who asked Carolina out on a date?
4. What was she thinking about while they were dancing?

A. While

Examples	Notes
While + past continuous tense, + past continuous tense **While** Andre **was becoming** successful, Carolina **was having** a hard time. **While** Andre **was making** a lot of friends, Carolina **wasn't meeting** anyone.	*While* is often used to connect two actions in the past that were happening at the same time.
Past continuous tense + *while* + past continuous tense Andre **was becoming** successful **while** Carolina **was having** a hard time. Carolina **wasn't meeting** anyone **while** Andre **was making** a lot of friends.	Use a comma only when *while* is at the beginning of the sentence.

1 Circle all the uses of *while* in Carolina's story on page 168. Underline all the verbs in those sentences. Tell what tense each verb is.

2 Complete these sentences with the correct pronouns.

1. While Carolina was living in Connecticut, _she_ was taking the train to Manhattan.

2. While Carolina was working as a waitress, _____ was earning a lot of money in tips.

3. Her customers were enjoying the music while _____ were enjoying a fine meal.

4. While Carolina's parents were having dinner, _____ were talking about Andre and her.

5. While Andre was living in San Francisco, _____ was meeting people from many countries.

6. Andre was eating at his desk while _____ was working.

7. Our teacher was writing on the board while _____ was explaining.

8. While I was doing my homework, _____ was listening to music.

3 Combine these pairs of sentences with *while*. If the subject of both sentences is the same, use a pronoun.

Example: Carolina was working in the restaurant. Carolina was meeting a lot of people.
   While Carolina was working in the restaurant, she was meeting a lot of people.

1. Andre was starting up his business. Andre was working hard.
2. Carolina was living with her aunt and uncle. Carolina wasn't working.
3. Andre was living in San Francisco. Andre was making new friends.
4. Carolina was working in the restaurant. Carolina wasn't speaking Portuguese.
5. Andre was living in San Francisco. Carolina was living in New York.
6. Carolina was studying hotel and restaurant management. Andre was studying computer technology.
7. We were working on Chapter 3. We were talking about friends and families.
8. Our teacher was giving us the homework assignment. We were packing up our books.

B. Past Continuous Tense Versus Simple Past Tense in Sentences with While

Use *while* with the past continuous tense to show the longer action. Use the simple past tense for the action that interrupts or stops the longer action. Use a comma only when *while* is at the beginning of the sentence.

While + past continuous tense, + simple past tense	Simple past tense + *while* + past continuous tense
While Carolina **was working,** she **met** an interesting young man. **While** she **was picking** up an order, he **asked** her for a date.	Carolina **met** an interesting young man **while** she **was working.** He **asked** her for a date **while** she **was picking** up an order.

4 Complete each sentence with the simple past tense or the past continuous tense of the verb in parentheses.

Example: While Andre was working in Chicago, he _decided_ (decide) to start his own business.

1. While Andre was planning his new business, he _____ (realize) San Francisco would be a perfect location.

2. While Andre was moving to San Francisco, he _____ (start) to feel nervous.

3. After one week in his new office he was beginning to think that he had made a mistake. While he was worrying, he _____ (receive) a phone call. It _____ (be) his first customer!

4. While he _____ (talk) to the customer, his pen ran out of ink.

5. While he was looking for another pen, the phone call _____ (be) disconnected.

6. Another customer came through the door while Andre _____ (try) to call the man back.

7. While he was talking to the new customer, the phone _____ (ring).

8. Another customer came into the office while he _____ (answer) the phone.

9. While Andre _____ (introduce) himself to the newest customer, he received a fax.

10. Two hours later, while he _____ (have) lunch, Andre decided that he needed an assistant.

5 Join the following pairs of sentences. Use *while*. If the subject is the same in both sentences, use a pronoun.

Example: Carolina was waiting on a table. Carolina saw two famous movie stars.
    While Carolina was waiting on a table, she saw two famous movie stars.

1. Carolina was taking the order. Carolina tried to think of the actors' names.
2. Tom Cruise and his date were ordering. Tom Cruise and his date smiled at Carolina.
3. Carolina was writing down the order. Tom Cruise asked a question.
4. Carolina was answering. Carolina forgot a word in English.
5. Carolina was turning red. Tom Cruise laughed and said, "Thank you" in Portuguese.
6. Carolina was walking to the kitchen. Carolina saw another famous person.
7. Tom Cruise and his date were leaving the restaurant. Carolina saw a $100 tip on the table.
8. Carolina was picking up the tip. Carolina waved good-bye.

Using What You've Learned

6 **Information Gap.** Carolina and Andre have different schedules.

- One partner chooses A and the other B.
- Look at chart A or B below. Don't look at your partner's chart.
- Ask your partner what Carolina or Andre was doing at a particular time yesterday. Write down the information in the chart.

Example: A. What was Andre doing at 7:00 yesterday morning?
B. He was sleeping.
B. What was Carolina doing at 7:00 yesterday morning?
A. She was getting up.

Chart A

Carolina's Schedule	Andre's Schedule
7:00 A.M. get up	7:00 A.M. *He was sleeping.*
7:30 go to class	7:30
10:00 take a break	10:00
12:00 (noon) eat lunch	12:00 (noon)
4:00 P.M. go to work	4:00 P.M.
7:00 take a break	7:00
10:00 go home	10:00

Chart B

Andre's Schedule	Carolina's Schedule
7:00 A.M. sleep	7:00 A.M. *She was getting up.*
7:30 sleep	7:30
10:00 arrive at the office	10:00
12:00 (noon) meet with staff	12:00 (noon)
4:00 P.M. take a break	4:00 P.M.
7:00 work	7:00
10:00 have dinner	10:00

7 **Comparing Past Activities.** Look back at Activity 6. Compare your schedule yesterday with Andre's or Carolina's schedules.

Example: Student A. While Andre was sleeping, I was driving to school.
Student B. While Carolina was getting up, I was eating breakfast.

8 **Writing a Story.** Finish this story about Carolina. Add at least five sentences.

While Carolina was working, she met a very interesting young man. His name was

_____. While they were talking, he asked her to go out on a date. He wrote down her telephone number. Then _____

_____

_____

_____

_____

_____.

When you finish, read your story to your group. Which story do you like best?

PART 4   *When;* Contrast of Simple Past and Past Continuous Tenses

Setting the Context

Prereading Questions   Where is the woman in the picture? What is in her hand? Make a guess.

My Own Business

I remember that moment so well. It was one of the happiest moments in my life! Oh, excuse me. I should introduce myself first. My name is Kyong Ah Kim. I am President of Kim's Travel & Learn.

When I went to Australia two years ago, I was just planning to learn English and travel around the country. While I was studying, I had an   5
idea. I decided to start my own travel and study business. When I called my father, I was shaking with excitement. I was explaining my idea carefully when my father said, "Stop! Wait!" He liked my idea a lot, but he didn't want to discuss it on the telephone.

When I arrived at the airport in Seoul, my father was waiting for me.   10
The next day we went to his office to make plans. Two weeks later we were signing papers in the bank. A month after that we put the sign "Kim's Travel & Learn" on my office door. When we opened the door of my new office, my mother took photographs. What a wonderful day that was.   15

Check Your Understanding

1.   Who is Kyong Ah Kim?
2.   When did she go to Australia?
3.   What did she decide to do?
4.   Who was waiting for her at the airport in Seoul?

A. When

Examples	Notes
When + simple past tense + past continuous tense **When** the phone **rang, I was talking** to my brother. **When** I **saw** the fire, **I was walking** to work.	Use *when* with the simple past tense for the action that stops or interrupts the longer action. Use the past continuous tense with the longer action.

1 Circle all the uses of *when* in the reading on page 172. Underline all the verbs in those sentences. Tell what tense each verb is.

2 Complete these sentences with *when* or *while*.

Example: _While_ Kyong Ah was studying in Australia, she had an idea.

1. _____ Kyong Ah was planning her business, she was talking to friends in Australia and the United States.

2. _____ the first group of students left for Australia, Kyong Ah was feeling nervous but excited.

3. _____ the students arrived in Australia, the escort called Kyong Ah.

4. _____ the students were studying and traveling, they were having a good time.

5. _____ there was a problem, Kyong Ah took care of it.

6. Kyong Ah met many interesting people _____ she was traveling.

7. Kyong Ah hired an assistant _____ she needed help.

3 Join each pair of sentences. Use *when*. If the subject is the same in both sentences, remember to use a pronoun.

Example: Students traveled to Hawaii. Kyong Ah accompanied them.
   When students traveled to Hawaii, Kyong Ah accompanied them.

1. The students got off the plane in Honolulu. The students' homestay families were waiting.

   _____

2. Someone put a lei* around Kyong Ah's neck. Kyong Ah smiled and laughed.

   _____

3. Students went to the class. Students wore shorts.

   _____

4. Students were in class. Students were thinking about the beach.

   _____

_____

*A *lei* is a flower necklace.

5. It rained in the afternoon. There was a beautiful rainbow.

   _____

6. They had a long weekend. Kyong Ah arranged a trip to Maui, another Hawaiian island.

   _____

7. They arrived in Maui. The sun was shining.

   _____

8. They left. A volcano on the island of Hawaii was erupting.

   _____

4   Complete these sentences. Use the simple past or the past continuous tense.

1. When I decided to learn English, I _____.
2. When I finished elementary school, I _____.
3. When I woke up this morning, _____.
4. When I first met my classmates, _____.
5. While I was going home from school one day, _____.
6. While our teacher was talking, _____.
7. While the students were taking a test, _____.
8. While I was sleeping last night _____.

B. Simple Past Tense Versus Past Continuous Tense

Examples	Notes
Kyong Ah **got up** every day at 6:00.	Use the simple past tense for repeated action in the past.
Kyong Ah **went** to bed at 10:00.	Use the simple past tense for a short action at a specific time in the past.
Kyong Ah **was sleeping** at 11:00.	Use the past continuous tense for an action in progress in the past.

5   Circle the correct verbs in these sentences.

Example: Andre ((ate) / was eating) breakfast quickly at 6:00 every morning.

1. Andre (went / was going) to bed at 1:00 A.M. in Brazil.
2. Andre (slept / was sleeping) at 6:00 in the morning.
3. Andre (worked / was working) seven days a week in San Francisco.
4. Carolina (worked / was working) at 9:00 last night.
5. Carolina (serve / was serving) dinner when the lights went out.

6. The customers (ate / were eating) by candlelight while the manager was calling an electrician.

7. Kyong Ah (traveled / was traveling) to Europe last summer.

8. The students (studied / were studying) four hours every day.

6 Use the past continuous tense when possible. Remember, some verbs are never used in continuous tenses. (See page 75.) Complete these readings with the correct forms of the verbs in parentheses.

Kyong Ah _was working_ (work) very hard. In fact, she was working seven days a

week, but she _____ (know) that it _____ (be) necessary. She
                1   2

_____ (work) eight to ten hours a day, but she _____ (understand)
       3   4

that she had to. She _____ (love) her job because it _____ (be)
                       5   6

all so challenging and new. She _____ (grow) more and more confident. At
                                7

first her parents _____ (be) very proud of her. Then they _____
                  8   9

(get) a little worried. They _____ (want) their daughter to be successful, but
                            10

they also _____ (feel) that it was time for her to get married.
         11

7 Complete these readings with the correct form of the verbs in parentheses. Use these tenses: simple present, present continuous, simple past, or past continuous.

1. When Andre _started_ (start) to study computers, he _____ (know) he
                                                 1

wanted a career working with technology. When he _____ (got) a job offer in
                                          2

San Francisco, he _____ (take) it. While he _____ (work) for the com-
                      3   4

pany, he _____ (plan) his own company.
        5

Now, ten years later Andre _____ (be) a successful owner of a growing com-
                                6

pany. He _____ (live) in San Francisco and he _____ (love) it. Now 20
         7   8

people _____ (work) for the company. They _____ (say) that he is a great boss.
       9   10

2. While Carolina _____ (live) in Connecticut, she _____ (not be) happy. When
                        1   2

she _____ (move) into the dormitory, her life _____ (get) better. While she _____
       3   4   5

(live) and _____ (work) in New York, she _____ (make) a lot of good friends.
         6   7

Now, ten years later, she _____ (be) back in Brazil. She _____ (man-
                              8   9
age) a restaurant in a large hotel. She _____ (earn) a good salary and
                                              10
_____ (enjoy) her job. Every year she _____ (travel) back to New York.
        11   12
Sometimes her friends from New York _____ (visit) her in Brazil.
                                          13

    3.   While Kyong Ah _____ (build) her company, she _____ (work)
                              1   2
a lot. She _____ (not date). She _____ (not relax). Her parents
              3   4
_____ (begin) to worry about her.
        5

Now, ten years later, she _____ (live) in Italy. She _____ (meet) an
                              6   7
Italian man and they _____ (fall) in love and _____ (get) married. They
                          8   9
_____ (live) in Korea for two years and then they _____ (move) to Italy.
    10   11
Kyong Ah _____ (speak) Italian well, but with an accent. They _____
              12   13
(be) very happy, but her parents _____ (not like) her being so far away.
                                      14

Using What You've Learned

8   **Talking About People.**

- Each person chooses one of the two people in the pictures below and on the next
  page to talk about.
- Make notes in the box next to the picture you choose.
- Take turns and tell a story about him or her. Tell about the person's life five years
  ago. Then tell about his or her life now.
- When you finish, join another pair of students. Tell one another about the people.
  Compare your stories.

Name:	City/Country:
Five years ago:	**Now:**

Name:	City/Country:
Five years ago:	**Now:**

Video Activities: Dentist Fashion Designer

Before You Watch.

1.   Match the careers in A with the descriptions in B.

A	B
_____ 1. fashion designer	a. takes pictures
_____ 2. dentist	b. paints pictures
_____ 3. photographer	c. makes clothes
_____ 4. artist	d. fixes teeth

2.   Which of the careers above is different from the others? Why?

Watch.   Check all the correct answers.

1.   Steve Schneider is a _____.

   a. _____ dentist   b. _____ photographer   c. _____ fashion designer

2.   Steve Schneider _____.

   a.   _____ likes dentistry as much as fashion design

   b.   _____ doesn't like having two careers

   c.   _____ started designing clothes in college

Watch Again.

1.   Steve Schneider has designed clothes for

   _____ Arnold Schwarzennegger

   _____ Bruce Springsteen

   _____ Tom Cruise

   _____ Sharon Stone

2. Put a *D* next to the benefit of being a dentist. Put an *F* next to the benefit of being a fashion designer.

    _____ Make more money.

    _____ Talk to people.

    _____ Work alone.

After You Watch.   Complete the sentences with the correct form of the verb. Use the past simple or the past continuous.

When I was young, I _decided_ (decide) to be a doctor. While I _____ (study) medicine, I _____ (start) working for an artist. At first, I just _____ (answer) the telephone and _____ (clean up). In my free time, I _____ (paint) just for fun. Then, one day while I _____ (paint), a customer _____ (come) into the studio. She _____ (see) my paintings and she _____ (like) them. Soon, I _____ (become) a part-time artist too.

Chapter 8

Food and Nutrition

| PART 1 |

Count Nouns; *Some* and *Any;* Questions with *How many; A, An*

Setting the Context

Prereading Questions   Where are these people? What are they eating?

What Are People Eating?

Nowadays people around the world are changing their eating habits. For example, it is common to see people in the United States eating sushi and Asians eating hamburgers and fries. Drinking a cup of coffee every day is now common in many parts of the world.

Where people eat is also changing. You can see fast food restaurants and   5
takeout counters in many places. Cafes and coffee shops are also located in many places. Walk around an airport in any major city of the world and you can find many of the same fast food choices.

Supermarkets in many countries offer shoppers foods from around the world. Travel is faster, so fresh fruits and vegetables appear everywhere. People around   10
the world know about different kinds of food and drink from television, movies, music, and the Internet.

Check Your Understanding

1.   Give examples from the reading to show that people are changing their eating habits.
2.   Give examples of some common fast food restaurants and takeout services.
3.   What is your favorite food? What is your favorite drink?

A. Count Nouns

A noun names a person, place, thing, idea, or emotion. There are two basic types of nouns—count nouns and noncount nouns. Count nouns are things you can count, such as chairs and people. Noncount nouns are things you can't count, such as water and air.

Examples		Notes
Singular	**Plural**	
box	boxes	Count nouns have singular and plural forms. (See Chapter 1 for spelling rules for -s endings.)
city	cities	
customer	customers	
shelf	shelves	

Common Irregular Count Nouns

Examples		Notes
Singular	**Plural**	
box	people	(See Chapter 1 for a more complete list of irregular noun plurals.)
cchild	children	
cwoman	women	
man	men	

1 Write the plurals of these count nouns.

1. person   *people*
2. woman
3. party
4. child
5. orange
6. box
7. radio
8. baby
9. goose
10. wife
11. church
12. apple
13. mouse
14. loaf
15. cherry
16. dish
17. man
18. tomato
19. shelf
20. foot

B. Some *and* Any *with Count Nouns*

	Examples	Notes
Questions	Do you have any apples or oranges at home?	Use *some* or *any* in questions.
	Would you like some apples?	
Affirmative Statement	I have some apples at home.	Use *some* in affirmative statements.
Negative Statement	I don't have any oranges at home.	Use *any* in negative statements.

2 Imagine that you are Mark or Linda below. Look at the picture of "your" kitchen, but not at your partner's picture. Ask questions about your partner's kitchen, using the ten cues below. Use *any* in your questions.

Examples: apples

    A.   Linda, do you have any
        apples?

    B.   Yes, I have some.

potato chips

    B.   Mark, do you have any potato
        chips?

    A.   No, I don't have any.

1. grapes
2. frozen dinners
3. oranges
4. potatoes
5. onions

6. bananas
7. canned tomatoes
8. carrots
9. peas
10. apples

C. Questions with How many

How many + count noun + auxiliary verb + subject + verb		
Questions	**Possible Answers**	**Notes**
How many bananas do you have?	I have three.	Use *how many* in questions with count nouns.
How many eggs do you need for the cake?	I need two.	

3 What do you eat each week? What do you drink? Take turns asking and answering questions with *how many* and the fifteen word cues on page 183.

Example: bananas

    A.   How many bananas do you eat each week?

    B.   I eat a banana almost every day.

    C.   I eat about two bananas a week.

    D.   I don't eat any bananas. I don't like them.

1. eggs
2. apples
3. glasses of milk
4. cookies
5. avocados
6. salads
7. ice cream cones
8. bags of potato chips
9. bottles of beer
10. cups of coffee
11. bowls of rice
12. oranges
13. hamburgers
14. cans of soda
15. sandwiches

D. A and An with Singular Count Nouns

Words Beginning with Consonant Sounds	Words Beginning with with Vowel Sounds	Notes
a banana **a** house **a** European* **a** supermarket	**an** egg **an** hour* **an** American **an** omelet	*A* and *an* mean "one" or "any." Use *a* before a consonant sound and *an* before a vowel sound. *Note that the sound is important, not the spelling.

4 Use *a* or *an* before each of these nouns.

1. _an_ apartment
2. _____ house
3. _____ egg
4. _____ banana
5. _____ orange
6. _____ apple
7. _____ hour
8. _____ European
9. _____ stove
10. _____ oven
11. _____ table
12. _____ knife

5 Complete this reading. Use *a* or *an* before singular nouns and put an × before plural nouns to show that no article is needed.

I'm Linda. Don't tell anybody, but I love fast food. I never make __*a*__ big breakfast. It takes too long. Instead I usually eat _____ bowl of _____ Chocoflakes. Occa-
₁   ₂
sionally I eat _____ egg for breakfast on the weekends. For a snack, I sometimes have
₃
_____ apple or _____ orange, but I like junk food better. I love potato chips, and _____
₄   ₅   ₆
pretzels. My favorite lunch is _____ hot dog or _____ hamburger, _____ french fries,
₇   ₈   ₉
and _____ big piece of chocolate cake. I don't cook lunch, of course! I always buy
₁₀

_____ lunches near work. My dinners are simple too. I usually have _____ microwave
   11   12

dinner or _____ can of spaghetti, _____ can of diet soda, and _____ ice cream sundae. I
            13   14   15

really have _____ terrible eating habits!
           16

6   Complete this conversation with _a, an, some,_ or _any._

Mark: We should go grocery shopping. We need __*some*__ things for dinner. I want to

make _____ omelet and _____ potatoes, but we don't have _____ potatoes. I
          1   2   3

want to make _____ apple pie too, but we don't have _____ apples. We also need
                   4   5

_____ cleaning supplies.
  6

Thomas: You're right. There's _____ broom, _____ vacuum cleaner, and _____
                               7   8   9

sponges here, but I don't see _____ cleaning supplies. By the way, who is going to
                                     10

clean?

Mark: I'm cooking, so that means you're cleaning.

Thomas: Hey, let's forget about shopping! I'd like _____ hamburger. Let's go out for
                                                        11

dinner, OK?

Using What You've Learned

7 **Talking About Food.** What food and household items do you have in your home?
Ask your partner questions with _any_ about things in your own homes. Give true answers. Use the cues from Activity 2 on page 182 and the words below. You can also
add your own words.

Example: _Do you have any tomatoes in your home?_

1. tomatoes
2. paper towels
3. frying pans
4. hot dogs
5. champagne glasses

6. sponges
7. knives
8. eggs
9. apples
10. coffee mugs

8 **Using a Questionnaire.** Find out what people in your class or community really eat.
Here's a questionnaire to help you. Ask three different people the questions. Add four
questions of your own. Then work in small groups and compare your answers.

HOW MANY DO YOU EAT OR DRINK EACH WEEK?			
1. How many cups of coffee or tea do you drink each week?			
2. How many apples, oranges, or bananas do you eat?			
3. How many salads do you eat?			
4. How many sandwiches do you eat? What kind?			
5. Do you eat any microwave meals? How many?			
6. How many times a week do you eat in fast food restaurants?			
7.			
8.			
9.			
10.			

PART 2 # Noncount Nouns; *Some* and *Any*

Setting the Context

Prereading Questions   Many people do not eat certain types of food. Look at the pictures below and describe them. Do you eat or drink these things?

I Don't Want Any, Thank You

There are different ideas about what you should eat. There are also many ideas about what you should *not* eat. Some of these ideas come from religion. For example, Muslims don't eat any pork because of their religion. Many Jews don't eat any pork either. Some Christians don't eat meat on Fridays. Other Christians don't drink any wine or coffee. Many Buddhists never eat any meat or eggs at all. They eat a lot of rice, beans, fruit, and nuts instead. Most Hindus also don't eat meat because they are vegetarians.

5

Check Your Understanding

1. Do Muslims eat pork?
2. Do some Jews eat pork?
3. What are some things Buddhists don't eat?
4. Do you know of any other rules about certain types of food?

A. Noncount Nouns

Noncount nouns can be ideas *(freedom)*, feelings *(love)*, activities *(golf)*, or things we measure *(oil)* or group together *(furniture)*. Noncount nouns are always singular. Do not add *-s* to these nouns, and do not use *a* or *an* with them.

Noncount Nouns			Count Nouns		
Examples		**Notes**	**Singular**	**Plural**	**Notes**
bread	flour	People usually measure these items.	apple	apples	People usually count these items.
butter	rice		banana	bananas	
coffee	tea		potato	potatoes	

1 Write *C* in front of count nouns and *N* in front of noncount nouns.

1. _C_ apple
2. ___ tomato
3. ___ rice
4. ___ cheese
5. ___ banana
6. ___ meat

7. ___ egg
8. ___ juice
9. ___ milk
10. ___ potato
11. ___ sugar
12. ___ sandwich

B. Some *and* Any *with Noncount Nouns*

	Examples	**Notes**
Questions	Would you like **some** tea?	Use *some* or *any* in questions.
	Do you have **any** coffee at home?	
Affirmative Statement	I have **some** Colombian coffee at home.	Use *some* in affirmative statements.
Negative Statement	I **don't** have **any** tea at home.	Use *any* in negative statements.

2 Write *some* or *any* in front of the following nouns.

Example: He doesn't want _any_ rice.

1. I would like _____ tea please.

2. They don't eat _____ meat.

3.   She needs _____ coffee to start the day.

4.   We don't have _____ juice in the refrigerator.

5.   You didn't buy _____ rice!

6.   He bought _____ cereal, but he couldn't find _____ chocolate mint ice cream.

7.   She prefers _____ sugar in her tea.

8.   I don't have _____ information on cooking fish.

3   Choose a shopping list from the two below. Make questions with *some* or *any*. Use the 12 words below. Ask each other a question about each word. Write down your partner's answers, but do not look at your partner's list. Can you guess what meal your partner is shopping for?

STUDENT A	STUDENT B
Shopping List	*Shopping List*
ice cream	butter
lettuce	tea
mustard	jam
ketchup	cheese
milk	sugar
rice	milk
coffee	coffee
meat	bread
	cereal

Examples: butter   butter
          A.   Do you need some butter?   B.   Do you need any butter?
          B.   Yes, I do.   A.   No, I don't.

1.   rice   5.   tea   9.   cereal
2.   milk   6.   mustard   10.   meat
3.   coffee   7.   jam   11.   ice cream
4.   sugar   8.   ketchup   12.   lettuce

4   You are having a party. Work in a chain. Ask and answer questions about the foods and drinks from the list on page 188. Use *some* in your questions. Remember to make count nouns plural. Give true answers.

Examples: soda   pretzel
          A.   Would you like some soda?
          B.   Yes, please.
          B.   Would you like some pretzels?
          C.   No, thanks.

1. potato chip	6. juice	11. cookie		
2. fresh vegetable	7. soda	12. fresh fruit		
3. dip	8. coffee	13. grape		
4. peanut	9. cream or sugar	14. watermelon		
5. popcorn	10. cake	15. apple		

Using What You've Learned

5   **Talking About Parties and Eating Habits.**   What do people in your family serve at a party or a special occasion? At an informal get-together? For a holiday? Take turns describing food at typical parties in your family. Use this chart to help you write your information.

Name				
Birthday parties				
Weddings				
_____ holiday (write the name of the holiday)				
Informal get-togethers				
Party to watch sporting event on TV				

PART 3

Counting Units and Units of Measurement; Questions with *How much*

Setting the Context

Prereading Questions   How old are these children? What countries do they come from? Make guesses.

Too Much and Not Enough

Many children in the United States have a new health problem. They are overweight, fat, or too heavy. Parents, doctors, schools, and the government want to fix this problem. Why do so many children weigh too much? Many children eat a lot of junk food and they do not get enough exercise. Video games and computers interest some children more than sports and outside games.   5

While some children are gaining weight, other children do not have enough food to eat. Hunger is a very serious problem in the United States and around the world. Some families do not have much money for food. How   10 many children go to school without breakfast? How many children go to bed without dinner? Unfortunately, the answer is too many.

Check Your Understanding

1.   What is a problem for many children in the United States?
2.   In general, do children in the United States get a lot of exercise?
3.   Do all families in the United States have money for food?
4.   According to the reading, is hunger a problem in the United States?

Hunger is a problem in many countries. Many people around the world don't have enough food to eat. What is being done to solve the problem of hunger? What more could be done, in your opinion?

A. Common Counting Units

Counting units are used with many kinds of food and household items. *Of* follows all these expressions except *dozen.* In measurement and recipes, other units are also used, such as *yards* and *teaspoons.* (See page 191 for a chart of these.)

bag	flour, potatoes, potato chips, sugar, etc.
bar	candy, hand soap, etc.
bottle	detergent, ketchup, juice, soda, and other liquids
box	cereal, laundry detergent, etc.
bunch	bananas, carrots, grapes, green onions, flowers, etc.
can	soda, soup, vegetables, tuna, etc.
carton	eggs, ice cream, milk, etc.
dozen	eggs, donuts
gallon, quart, pint	all liquids, ice cream, yogurt
head	cabbage, cauliflower, lettuce
jar	jam, mayonnaise, mustard, peanut butter, etc.
loaf	bread
package	cookies, potato chips, spaghetti, etc.
piece	bread, cake, meat, cheese, etc.
pound, ounce	cheese, meat, poultry, fruits, vegetables, etc.
roll	paper towels, toilet paper, etc.
tube	toothpaste, hand cream, etc.

1   Write the correct counting unit under the picture of each type of food below. Some foods can have more than one counting unit.

_a_ _bag_	___ _____	___ _____	___ _____	___ _____
of sugar	of soda	of soup	of milk	eggs
___ _____	___ _____	___ _____	___ _____	___ _____
of lettuce	of pickles	of bread	of cheese	of cheese

2   Complete this grocery list.

Don't Forget		
1. one _gallon_____ of milk		7. one _____ of lettuce
2. one _____ of potatoes		8. two _____ of toothpaste
3. two _____ of green onions		9. three _____ of hand soap
4. one _____ of mayonnaise		10. two _____ of bananas
5. three _____ of butter		11. one _____ of laundry detergent
6. one _____ eggs		12. one _____ of oil

3   Change the eight items below on the left from metric units of measurement to basic units of measurement. Use the chart on the right to help you.

Example: four liters of gas

Four liters of gas is about one gallon of gas.

Metric Units

1.   four liters of milk
2.   ten centimeters of tape
3.   one liter of juice
4.   two meters of string
5.   one kilo of chicken
6.   500 grams of coffee
7.   five kilometers
8.   18 degrees Celsius

Basic Units	
Length	meter = about 1.1 yards
	centimeter = .01 meter = about .4 inch
	kilometer = 1,000 meters = about .6 mile
Volume	liter = about 1.06 quarts (4 quarts = 1 gallon)
	milliliter = 0.001 liter
	5 milliliters = 1 teaspoon
Weight	30 grams = 1.1 ounces
	kilogram = 1,000 grams = 2.2 pounds
Temperature	Celsius: 0°C = 32°F
	37°C = 98.6 °F

B. Questions with How much

Form	*How much* + noncount noun + auxiliary verb + subject + verb	
Questions and Possible Answers		**Notes**
How much bread should I buy? Buy two loaves of bread, please. **How much sugar** do we need? We need at least two bags.		Use *how much* in questions with noncount nouns.

4 Look at the pictures below. How much of each ingredient do you need? Take turns asking and answering questions with *how much*.

Example: ice cream
   A.   How much ice cream do I need?
   B.   You need two scoops of ice cream.

1.

Ice cream sundae
- ice cream
- chocolate sauce
- whipped cream

2.

Spaghetti for one
- cooked spaghetti
- spaghetti sauce
- grated cheese

3.

Smoothie
- juice
- banana
- protein powder

4.
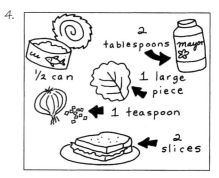

Tuna sandwich
- bread
- tuna
- chopped onion
- mayonnaise
- lettuce

5 Make fried rice for dinner. Look at page 193. Student A looks at the list of ingredients. Ask Student B questions about the ingredients. Then Student B looks at the recipe card and answers Student A's questions.

Example: Oil
   A.   How much oil do we need?
   B.   We need four tablespoons.

STUDENT A

Ingredients	
1. rice	5. celery
2. soy sauce	6. carrots
3. garlic	7. eggs
4. onions	8. chicken

STUDENT B

Chinese-American Fried Rice (4 People)

4 tablespoons of soy sauce
2 teaspoons of mashed garlic
4 tablespoons of oil
1 small onion, chopped
2 stalks of celery, chopped
2 carrots, chopped
2 eggs, beaten
4 cups of cooked rice

Optional Ingredients

1 cup of beef, chicken, pork, or seafood, cut in strips

Mix soy sauce and garlic, set aside. Heat a frying pan and add oil. Fry any optional ingredients. Fry the rest of the ingredients in the order listed. Add rice and fry for two minutes. Add soy sauce and garlic. Fry for two more minutes. Serve hot.

Using What You've Learned

6 **Playing a Memory Game.** Work in a chain. One student begins by saying, "We need *a bottle of ketchup*." The next student repeats the first item and adds one. Every student must repeat the list and add one item.

Example: A. We need a bottle of ketchup.
B. We need a bottle of ketchup and a dozen eggs.
C. We need a bottle of ketchup, a dozen eggs, and . . .

7 **Explaining Recipes.** Choose a favorite but simple recipe. Write a list of ingredients and directions for making it. Explain your recipe to your partner and read the list of ingredients. Share your recipes with the class. Plan an international dinner if you wish!

| PART 4 | # Common Noncount Nouns; *A lot (of)*; *A little* Versus *A few*; *Not many* Versus *Not much* |

Setting the Context

Prereading Questions   Look at the different types of food in the picture. Do you eat and drink them?

I'll Have a "Lite" Please

Nowadays many people are eating "lite" food. "Lite" food has less fat. People are changing their eating habits and choosing "lite" food because it is not healthy to eat a lot of fat. As a result, supermarkets are carrying many kinds of low-fat products.

    A good example of these changes is milk. In the past, everyone drank whole milk. Nowadays, except for small children, not many people drink whole milk.   5 Most adults drink two percent, one percent, or skim milk. There is a little fat in two percent and one percent milk, but skim milk has no fat.

    Milk is only one example. Just take a look in a few supermarkets. You will see "lite" food on every shelf. More and more, supermarkets are selling—and shoppers are buying—low-fat, nonfat, lean, diet, or "lite" food.   10

Check Your Understanding

1.   What is "lite" food?
2.   Why are many people choosing "lite" food these days?
3.   What kinds of milk can you find in supermarkets?

Many people today are very careful about fat in their diets. Do you worry about fat? Cholesterol? Do you try to eat healthy foods and get exercise?

A. More Noncount Nouns

advice	jewelry	pollution	bowling
clothing	laundry	time	cleaning
crime	mail	traffic	cooking
furniture	money	transportation	sewing
help	music	weather	swimming
homework	paper	work	tennis
information			

Note: Some nouns such as *time* can be count or noncount nouns.
COUNT   I went there **many times.**
NONCOUNT   I have **some free time** this afternoon.

B. A lot (of)

Examples		Notes
Count Nouns	**Noncount Nouns**	
I have a **lot of quarters** with me.	I have **a lot of change** with me.	Use *a lot of* with both count and noncount nouns.
Does he have **a lot?**	Does he have **a lot?**	Use *a lot* without a noun.
He doesn't have **a lot.**	He doesn't have **a lot.**	

1 Ask and answer questions with these cues. Give true answers. Be careful with verb tense.

Example: eat / junk food
　　　　A. Do you eat a lot of junk food?
　　　　B. Yes, I do eat a lot of junk food.
　　　or No, I don't eat a lot.

1. eat / fruit
2. eat / vegetables yesterday
3. drink / coffee
4. spend / money last week
5. get / mail last week
6. have / English-speaking friends
7. have / problems
8. have / furniture in your home

C. A Little *Versus* A few; Not many *Versus* Not much

Examples		Notes
With Count Nouns		
Do you have **many quarters** with you?		Use *many* in questions with plural count nouns.
I have **a few quarters.**	(I have a small number, perhaps enough.)	Use *a few* and *not many* in statements with plural count nouns.
I don't have **many quarters** with me.	(I have a small number, probably not enough.)	
With Noncount Nouns		
Do you have **much change** with you?		Use *much* in questions with noncount nouns.
I have **a little change.**	(I have a small amount, perhaps enough.)	Use *a little* and *not much* in statements with noncount nouns.
I don't have **much change.**	(I have a small amount, probably not enough.)	

2   Use + *(some)* or − *(not enough)* to show the difference in meaning in these sentences.

Examples: ___+___ She has a little money.

          ___−___ She doesn't have much money.

1. _____ We have a little food at home.

    _____ We don't have much juice.

2. _____ There are a few apples.

    _____ We don't have many oranges.

3. _____ She has a few friends.

    _____ He doesn't have many friends.

4. _____ We don't have much furniture in our apartment.

    _____ They have a few chairs.

5. _____ He doesn't have much homework tonight.

    _____ She has a few homework assignments tonight.

6. _____ She got a little information on the Internet.

    _____ I didn't get much information on the Internet.

7. _____ They don't have many questions.

    _____ He has a few questions.

8. _____ I needed a little help.

    _____ She didn't need much help.

3 Complete this reading. Circle the correct words in parentheses. Circle ✕ if no word is needed.

Diet and Eating Habits

Around the world, people's eating habits are changing. In many ways, this is

unfortunate. Traditional diets are often more healthy. For example, a traditional

Japanese meal includes (a lot /(a lot of)) rice and vegetables and (a / a little)
1

fish. A traditional Mexican meal includes (some / a little) beans and rice and
2

(a few / a little) tortillas. (A / X) traditional Italian meal includes (some / a few) fruit,   5
3   4   5

(some / a little) vegetables, and (a lot of / many) pasta. All of these diets include
6   7

(a / X) healthy food.
8

    But traditional diets are changing. People in Tokyo, Mexico City, Rome, and

(many / much) other parts of the world are changing their eating habits. Today,
9

(a / X) hamburgers, hot dogs, and french fries are common around the world.   10
10

People are eating (a lot of / a) white bread instead of traditional food such as
11

Colombian *arepas* or Mexican *tortillas.*

    In the United States, diets are changing too. Hopefully, the American diet will

be better. In the past, (a / X) traditional American dinner included (a lot of / a few)
12   13

meat, (much/some) potatoes, and (a few/a little) vegetables. Today Americans   15
         14   15

aren't eating as (many/much) meat as in the past. They are adding (some/any)
               16   17

beans and tofu to their meals. They are also trying to eat (a few/a little) fruit or
                                           18

(a few/a little) vegetables at every meal. But Americans still eat (a lot of/many)
   19   20

junk food too.

Using What You've Learned

4   **Discussing Diets.**   Discuss these questions in a small group. Then choose one student to tell the class about the discussion.

1.   What was the traditional diet of your parents or grandparents?
2.   How is your diet changing?
3.   What is your opinion about these changes?

5   **Discussing World Records.**   Read the following information from *Guinness World Records 2000,* Bantam Books, by Guinness Publishing Ltd. pages 92 to 94.

Largest Sushi Roll   Six hundred members of the Nikopoka Festa committee made a sushi roll (kappamaki) that was 3,279 ft. long at Yoshii, Japan, on October 12, 1997.
Biggest Restaurant Steak   A 12 lb.8oz. rump steak (precooked weight) is available at the Kestrel Inn, Hatton, England. It takes about 40 minutes to cook and costs $128. If a customer finishes the steak, the management will make a donation to charity.
Biggest Bowl of Spaghetti   On August 16, 1998, a bowl of spaghetti weighing 605 lbs. was cooked by Consolidated Communication in London, England, on behalf of Disney Home Video to celebrate the rerelease of the movie, Lady and the Tramp.
Biggest Hamburger   The biggest hamburger ever weighed 2.5 tons and was made at the Outagimie County Fairgrounds in Seymour, Wisconsin, on August 5, 1989.
Biggest Ice Cream Sundae   On July 24, 1988, the biggest ice cream sundae ever, weighing 22.59 tons, was put together by Palm Dairies Ltd. Alberta, Canada. The finished concoction included 18.38 tons of ice cream, 3.98 tons of syrup, and 537 lb.3oz. of topping.

Make four questions for your partner to answer.

Examples: *How long was the largest sushi roll? Who made the largest sushi roll?*

■   Ask your partner questions and answer your partner's questions.

■   Look in the library or on the Internet for more world food records to tell your class.

Checking Your Progress

Check your progress with structures from Chapters 7 and 8. Be sure to review any problem areas.

Part 1.   Choose the correct word(s) to complete each sentence.

1. Antonietta _____ a wonderful idea while she was riding the bus.
   a. have
   b. has
   c. had
   d. having
   e. is having

2. When the doorbell rang, I _____ out of my seat.
   a. was jumping
   b. jump
   c. jumps
   d. jumped
   e. jumping

3. Students in a new school often need _____ advice.
   a. a lot of
   b. many
   c. a lot
   d. a few
   e. lots

4. There weren't _____ people in the classroom, so it was easy to find a good seat.
   a. much
   b. some
   c. a few
   d. many
   e. a lot

5. While Juan and Silvia _____ to class last night, they saw an accident.
   a. walking
   b. walked
   c. were walking
   d. walk
   e. are walking

6. Pablo didn't have _____ eggs, so he couldn't bake a cake.
   a. any
   b. a little
   c. much
   d. a lot
   e. some

7. While Duc was studying, the telephone _____ two times.
   a. rings
   b. is ringing
   c. was ringing
   d. ring
   e. rang

8. I don't have any money, but Jean has _____.
   a. much
   b. a lot of
   c. many
   d. a few
   e. some

9. When I turned on the computer, the electricity _____ out.
   a. go
   b. went
   c. is going
   d. was going
   e. was gone

10. Mari's class has many international students, but my class has only _____.
    a. a lot
    b. a lot of
    c. a little
    d. any
    e. a few

Part 2.   Circle the correct words to complete this story.

When I was a child, my parents (wanted / were wanting) me to be healthy. They always
_____1

gave me (much / a lot of) milk, and they thought it was important to play in the sun.
_____2

Today, doctors have very different ideas about good health, (do / don't) they?
_____3

      Mother's (use / used) to give their babies "formula" and cow's milk. Now we be-
____4

lieve that mother's milk is better. In the past, parents also thought that children

(have / had) to eat meat every day. But many people do not eat (some / any) meat, and
___5   6

they are very healthy.

      Thirty years ago, (many / much) people would sit in the sun for good health. Today,
_____7

(a lot / a lot of) people stay away from the sun because of the danger of skin cancer.
___8

      In the past, many older people (do / did) not do (much / many) exercise, but today
_____9_____10

there are exercise programs for everyone. Because of these new ideas, people now

have longer and healthier lives.

Video Activities: Diets

Before You Watch.

1.   People on diets usually want to _____.

     a. lose weight   b. gain weight   c. get stronger

2.   Check the foods that people on restrictive diets usually cannot eat.

     _____ ice cream   _____ fruit   _____ candy   _____ butter

     _____ vegetables   _____ chicken   _____ bread   _____ rice

Watch.

Vocabulary Note

A crash diet is very restrictive. People on crash diets are usually trying to lose
weight very quickly.

1.   Dr. Goodrick explains why restrictive diets are _____.

     a.   good for you

     b.   dangerous

     c.   necessary for some people

2. Check all of the things that Dr. Goodrick says a crash diet can do:

_____ change your brain chemistry

_____ help you stay thin

_____ make you want to eat more

_____ make you gain weight

Watch Again.

1. How long should it take to get used to a low-fat diet?

   a. almost 6 weeks   b. at least 6 months   c. about 6 days

2. Check all of the things that you should do to lose weight:

_____ eat only fruits and vegetables

_____ change your eating habits slowly

_____ eat fewer than 1,200 calories a day

_____ find friends to help you

_____ try new ways of cooking

_____ stop eating high-fat foods immediately

_____ plan your meals

_____ exercise

After You Watch. Complete the following conversation with *a little, a few, a lot (of), much,* or *many.*

A: I know I'm not fat but I'd like to lose _____ weight.

B: How _____ weight do you want to lose?

A: Just _____ kilos, maybe five or six. I'm trying not to eat

_____ fat or sugar. That's difficult for me because I usually eat

_____ cookies.

B: How _____ cookies do you eat in one day?

A: Maybe three or four.

B: How _____ exercise do you do?

A: _____. I run ten kilometers a day.

Chapter 9

Great Destinations

<table>
<tr><td>**PART 1**</td><td># Adjectives with *-ing* and *-ed;*
Go Versus *Play; It's* +
Adjective + Infinitive</td></tr>
</table>

Setting the Context

Prereading Questions   Where is the young couple in this picture? How old do you think they are?

A New Campus

Hi. My name is Josh. I'm a student. I grew up in Naples, Florida. I studied biology at the community college there for two years. I still study biology, but I'm not in Florida anymore. I'm at the University of Texas at Austin. We call it UT.

My life is different here—very different. For one thing, UT is much bigger than my old community college. And Austin is a lot more exciting than Naples. It's great   5
to go out at night here. I mean there are just more things to do—more movies, more music, more parties.

Yeah, this is an interesting place, and I am never bored, but I still miss home.

Check Your Understanding   Circle T for *True* or F for *False*. Correct the false sentences.

1.   T F Josh used to live in Naples, Florida.
2.   T F UT is smaller than his old community college.
3.   T F Austin is more exciting than Naples.
4.   T F It's great to stay home at night.
5.   T F Josh is never bored.

It is common for college students in the United States to study far from their homes. It is also common to start at one college and then transfer to another. How many different schools have you gone to?

1 Complete this reading with the present, past, and past continuous tenses of the verbs in parentheses.

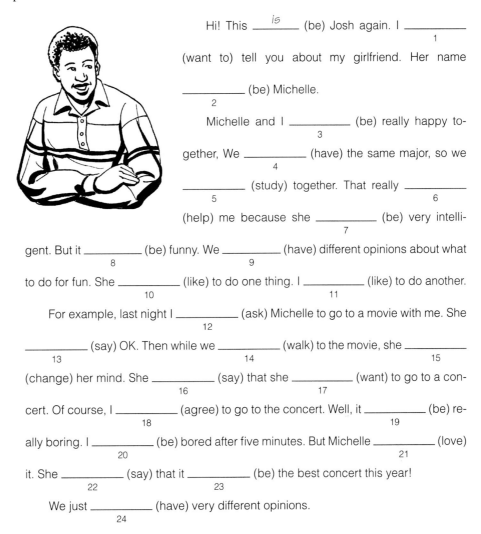

Hi! This ___*is*___ (be) Josh again. I _____ (want to) tell you about my girlfriend. Her name _____ (be) Michelle.
    1
    2

Michelle and I _____ (be) really happy to-gether. We _____ (have) the same major, so we _____ (study) together. That really _____ (help) me because she _____ (be) very intelli-gent. But it _____ (be) funny. We _____ (have) different opinions about what to do for fun. She _____ (like) to do one thing. I _____ (like) to do another.
    3
    4
    5
    6
    7
    8
    9
    10
    11

For example, last night I _____ (ask) Michelle to go to a movie with me. She _____ (say) OK. Then while we _____ (walk) to the movie, she _____ (change) her mind. She _____ (say) that she _____ (want) to go to a con-cert. Of course, I _____ (agree) to go to the concert. Well, it _____ (be) re-ally boring. I _____ (be) bored after five minutes. But Michelle _____ (love) it. She _____ (say) that it _____ (be) the best concert this year!
    12
    13
    14
    15
    16
    17
    18
    19
    20
    21
    22
    23

We just _____ (have) very different opinions.
    24

A. Adjectives with -ing and -ed

Adjectives with *-ing* and *-ed* often follow *to be.*

Examples		Notes
Giver ⟶ Receiver		
The movie **excited** Josh.	The movie was **exciting.**	Use *-ing* with the *giver* of a feeling.
	Josh was **excited.**	
Giver Receiver		
Dave **bores** Michelle.	Dave is **boring.**	Use *-ed* with the *receiver* of a feeling.
	Michelle is **bored.**	

2 Change each underlined verb to an adjective. Use the *-ed* or *-ing* form of the adjective to complete the sentences.

I'm Michelle. Josh told you we often have different opinions on things.
Well, it's true. For example:

1. We watched a TV show last night.

    It excited me. For me, the show was ___exciting.___ I was ___excited.___

    It bored Josh. For Josh, the show was _____. He was _____.

2. We both read the same book.

    The book fascinated me. I was _____. For me, the book was _____.

    The book shocked Josh. He was _____. For him, the book was

    _____.

3. We went to eat at a restaurant.

    The food disappointed me. For me, the food was _____. I was

    _____.

    The food satisfied Josh. For him, the food was _____. He was _____.

4. We went to a football game.

    The game confused me. I was _____. To me, the game was _____.

    The game excited Josh. He was _____. To Josh, the game was _____.

5. We went to hear a politician speak.

    The politician surprised me. To me, the politician was _____. I was _____.

    The politician didn't interest Josh. To Josh, the politician was not _____.

    Josh was not _____.

3 Here's one thing Josh and I agree on. It's fun to watch people, especially in our classes. It's entertaining, and it doesn't cost anything!

Look at the pictures below and on page 207. Then answer the questions using the *-ing* or *-ed* forms of the adjectives.

Example: Who is bored?
The students are bored.

Ms. Hanson

Mr. Mosca

1. Who is bored?
    Who is boring?

2. Who is interesting?
    Who is interested?

3. Who was fascinated?   **4.** Who was disappointed?   **5.** Who is surprised?
Who was fascinating?   What was disappointing?   What is surprising?

6. Is the food disappointing or disappointed? Is Josh disappointing or disappointed?

7. Is the book confused or confusing? How about Harry?

8. Is this grammar point confused or confusing for you?

B. Using Go with an Activity; Using Play with Games and Sports

Form	Go + verb + -ing
Examples	**Notes**
I **go dancing** every Saturday night. I **went shopping** yesterday. I'm going to **go jogging** tomorrow.	When the verb *go* is followed by an activity, the activity ends in *-ing*.

Form	Subject + play + game or sport
Examples	**Notes**
Let's **play** tennis. I **play** cards almost every night.	When the verb *play* is followed by the name of a game or sport, the *-ing* ending is *not* used.

4 Follow the pattern below with a partner. Use *go* or *play* in your answers. Change roles.

Example: football / bowl

A.   What do you want to do this afternoon?

B.   Let's play football.

A.   No, let's go bowling.

1. shop / tennis
2. roller-skate / chess
3. Ping-Pong / ski
4. jog / checkers
5. surf / baseball

6.   soccer / sightsee
7.   dance / basketball
8.   soccer / walk
9.   run / cards
10. volleyball / window shop

C. It's + *Adjective* + *Infinitive*

People often use this pattern to give an opinion about an activity or game.

Examples	Notes
It's great to play cards. **It's boring to go** jogging. **It's terrible to be** sick.	Adjectives such as *fascinating, exciting, interesting,* and *tiring* are commonly used in this pattern.

5 Look at the following list of ten activities. Give your opinion of these activities by checking the appropriate boxes. Then work with a partner. Take turns making sentences. In your sentences, you can also use words like *sometimes, usually, always,* and *never.*

Example: to stay home

It's sometimes boring to stay home because there's nobody to talk with.

	Great	Fantastic	Fun	Boring	Tiring	Terrible
1. to stay home				✓		
2. to watch TV						
3. to go shopping						
4. to read a book						
5. to go to a museum						
6. to go to a concert						
7. to play tennis						
8. to surf the Internet						
9. to go to a party						
10. to hang out with friends						

Using What You've Learned

6 **Giving Opinions.**   Write six things that you often do. Then, in a small group, share your opinions of each other's activities. Use *it's interesting / boring / fascinating,* and so on. Give the reason for your opinion.

Example: hiking*

In my opinion, it's fascinating to go hiking because I love nature.

1. _____

2. _____

3. _____

4. _____

5. _____

6. _____

PART 2

Would rather; Comparative Adjectives

Setting the Context

Prereading Questions   Look at the picture. What is the man thinking about?

Decisions, Decisions

Dale: Hey, Jack. I heard you and Julie sold your business.

Jack: Yeah, we want to take some time off. There are more interesting things to do than just work.

Dale: What are you going to do?

Jack: Travel, but we can't decide between Italy and France, I'd rather go to France than Italy. Julie would rather visit Italy. Hey, you know Europe well. What do you think?

_____

*Hiking—walking in the mountains or woods for fun.

Dale: Well, I love both countries. But in my opinion, Italy has better museums than France, and it's usually cheaper. Also, Italian is easier to speak than French. On the other hand, France has more beautiful churches than Italy. And I think French food is a little better than Italian.

Jack: So which country should we visit?

Dale: Both!

Check Your Understanding   Circle T for *True* or F for *False*. Correct the false sentences.

1.   T F Jack just bought a new business.
2.   T F Jack wants to go to Italy, not France.
3.   T F Julie doesn't agree with Jack.
4.   T F Dale thinks Italy has more museums than France.
5.   T F Dale thinks France has more churches than Italy.

A. Would rather

Use *would rather* if there is a choice. *Would rather* shows preference.

Examples	Notes
Would you rather visit China or Japan? **I'd (I would) rather** visit Japan. **Would they rather** come tonight or tomorrow? **They'd (They would) rather** come tonight (than tomorrow).	In statements, *would* is usually shortened (*I'd, He'd, They'd, etc.*). *Than* may be used to show the choice you do not prefer.

1   Imagine you are like Jack. You have free time and a lot of money. Use *would rather* to answer these questions.

Example: Would you rather go to France or Italy?
> *I'd rather go to France (than Italy).*

1.   Would you rather speak French or Italian?
2.   Would you rather visit Thailand or Singapore?
3.   Would you rather see Brazil or Peru?
4.   Would you rather eat Mexican food or American food?
5.   Would you rather go to Spain or Morocco?
6.   Would you rather read a book or watch a movie?
7.   Would you rather study more or take a break?
8.   Would you rather listen to jazz or rock and roll?

2   Take turns asking and answering the following questions with *would rather.* Use the cues to form the questions. Then add questions of your own.

Example: learn Arabic or English
          A.   Would you rather learn Arabic or English?
          B.   I'd rather learn Arabic.

1. see a rock concert or an opera
2. live in Spain or Portugal
3. play soccer or _____
4. visit Egypt or _____
5. eat _____ or _____

6. watch _____ or _____
7. _____ _____ or _____
8. _____ _____ or _____
9. _____ _____ or _____
10. _____ _____ or _____

B. Comparative Adjectives (1)

Comparatives show how two things are different. The form of the comparative depends on how many syllables the adjective has.

	Examples	Notes
One-Syllable Adjectives	France isn't **cheap.** Italy is **cheaper than** France.	Add *-er* to one-syllable adjectives. Use *than* to show the other choice.
Adjectives That End in *y*	French isn't **easy.** Italian is **easier** (to learn) **than** French.	When adjectives end in *y*, change the *y* to *i* and add *-er.*

3 Jack and Julie are going to visit both France and Italy. Which cities should they visit? Study the map of France below and use your imagination. Then use the adjectives below to make sentences comparing the cities.

In France—Paris or Nice?

Example: cool

  Paris is cooler than Nice.

1. warm
2. noisy
3. green
4. big
5. small

6. close (to the ocean)
7. sunny
8. cloudy
9. near (to England)

C. Comparative Adjectives (2)

Longer adjectives use *more . . . than* to form the comparative.

	Examples	Notes
Two-Syllable Adjectives That Don't End in *y*	This map is **more helpful than** that one. She is **more tired than** Jack.	Use *more . . . than* with these adjectives. Don't add *-er*.
Adjectives with More Than Two Syllables	The mountains are **more beautiful than** the beach.	Use *more . . . than* with these adjectives. Don't add *-er*.

4   What about Italy? Which Italian cities should Jack and Julie visit? Read what the travel agent has to say. Then use the adjectives below to make sentences comparing Florence and Rome.

In Italy—Florence or Rome?

Example: beautiful

Florence is more beautiful than Rome.

Rome is important, exciting, and interesting, but it is also crowded.

Florence is beautiful, relaxing, peaceful, and safe, but it is also very expensive.

1. exciting
2. safe
3. expensive
4. important
5. relaxing
6. interesting
7. crowded
8. peaceful
9. enjoyable

5   Choose two cities that both you and your partner know well. Then use these adjectives to compare the two cities. Add two adjectives of your own.

Write the names of the cities here: _____ and _____

1. beautiful
2. big
3. exciting
4. noisy
5. small
6. interesting
7. dangerous
8. smoggy
9. entertaining
10. wet
11.
12.

D. Irregular Comparative Adjectives

Some comparative adjectives do not follow the rules on pages 211 and 212. They are irregular. Here are three common examples.

Adjective ⟶ Comparative	Examples
good ⟶ better	Mary is **better than** Dave in sports.
bad ⟶ worse	Dave is **worse than** Mary in sports.
far ⟶ farther	Mary can run **farther than** Dave.

6   **Part 1.**   Jack and Julie finally decided to visit Paris and Florence, but how should they travel? Use the comparative forms of the verbs in parentheses to complete the conversation.

Jack: We know that we are going to Europe. But how should we get there? Is it _better_ (good) to sail or to fly?

Julie: For me, flying is _____ (good) than sailing.
                                            1

Jack: Why do you say that?

Julie: Flying is _____ (fast). It's also _____ (cheap), and it's
                           2   3
_____ (safe) than sailing.
         4

Jack: I disagree. For me, flying is _____ (bad) than sailing. Sailing may be
                                            5
_____ (slow) and _____ (expensive) than flying. But sailing is
         6   7
also _____ (interesting), and it's _____ (romantic).
           8   9

Part 2.   The conversation continues. Again fill in the correct comparative forms. But this time, finish the dialogue.

Jack: Should we travel by car or by train in Europe?

Julie: For me, the train is _____ (good) than the car.
                                  1

Jack: Why do you say that?

Julie: The train is _____ (good) because _____.
                               2   3

Jack: I disagree. For me, the train is _____ (bad) than the car.
                                                          4

The train is _____ (bad) because _____.
                         5   6

Using What You've Learned

7 **Talking About the World.**   How well do you know other countries? Fill in as many countries on the map as you can. Then use *closer* and *farther* to ask and answer questions about these cities with a partner.

Example: Which is farther from here, Australia or India?
    Australia is farther.

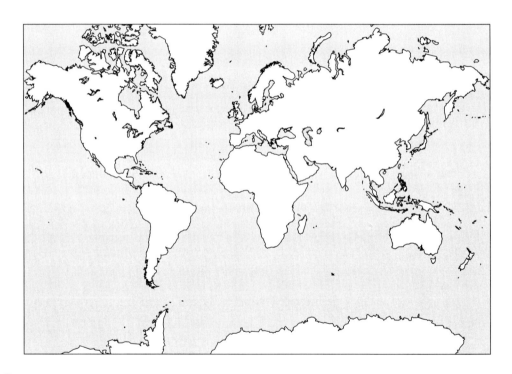

8 **Planning a Trip.**   You and a friend are planning a trip. However, you cannot agree on a place. You visit your travel agent and ask for help. Your travel agent can tell you the good points and bad points of each place. In groups of three—you, your friend, and the travel agent—role play this situation. Use one of the pairs of vacations below or choose your own.

1. a ski trip to Switzerland versus a sightseeing trip to New York City
2. an African safari versus a mountain-climbing expedition to Mount Everest
3. a backpacking trip in Nepal versus a luxury cruise on the Mediterranean

| PART 3 | # Adjectives Versus Adverbs; Comparative Adverbs; Comparisons with (*not*) As . . . *as* |

Setting the Context

Prereading Questions   What did the man in the picture just do? How old do you think he is?

The Prime of Life

My name is John Wilson. I'm a professor at a small university in Utah. My teaching schedule keeps me pretty busy, so I really enjoy my time away from work. What do I do for fun? Lots of things! I go to movies, plays, and concerts. I sing in a choir and play the piano. But more than anything, I love to exercise. That's my idea of entertainment!   5

  I love any kind of sport. I run, bicycle, ski, and play tennis, but basketball is my favorite. There is just one problem. I'm not as young as I used to be. I run more slowly than I used to. I can't jump as high. And I get hurt more easily. For all these reasons, I don't play as well as I did a few years ago. Oh well, I guess that's just part of getting older.   10

Check Your Understanding   Circle T for *True* or F for *False*. Correct the false sentences.

1.   T   F   John Wilson is musical.
2.   T   F   He enjoys exercise.
3.   T   F   He runs faster than he used to.
4.   T   F   He can't jump as high as he used to.
5.   T   F   He plays better than he used to.

A. Adjectives Versus Adverbs

	Examples	**Notes**
Adjectives	John is a **slow** runner. John is **slow**. Dave is a **fast** runner. Dave is **fast**.	Adjectives describe nouns.
Adverbs	John runs **slowly**. Dave runs **quickly**.	Adverbs describe actions. Most adverbs end in *-ly*.
One-Syllable Adverbs	Dave runs **fast**. He works **hard**. He worked **late** last night.	The words *fast, hard,* and *late* have the same form for adjective and adverb. Do *not* add *-ly*.
Irregular Adverbs	Susan is a **good** soccer player. Susan plays soccer **well**.	The correct adverb form of *good* is *well*.

1   Circle the correct forms, adjective or adverb, in the pairs of sentences.

1. John is a ((good)/ well) player. John plays basketball (good /(well)).
2. He is a (slow / slowly) runner. He runs (slow / slowly).
3. John jumps (good / well). He is a (good / well) jumper.
4. His voice is (soft / softly). He speaks (soft / softly).
5. John plays (careful / carefully). He is a (careful / carefully) player.
6. He doesn't play (dangerous / dangerously). He isn't a (dangerous / dangerously) player.
7. He is a (beautiful / beautifully) singer. He sings (beautiful / beautifully).
8. John walks (quiet / quietly). He is a (quiet / quietly) walker.
9. John gets hurt (easy / easily). It's (easy / easily) to hurt him.
10. John thinks (fast / fast). He is a (fast / fast) thinker.
11. John plays the piano (good / well). He is a (good / well) pianist.

B. Comparative Adverbs

Comparative adverbs show the difference between two actions. The form of the comparative depends on how many syllables the adverb has.

	Examples	**Notes**
One-Syllable Adverbs	John's son runs **faster than** John.	Use -er . . . than with these adverbs.
Adverbs with Two or More Syllables	John finished his work **more quickly than** Ben.	Use more (not -er) with these adverbs.
Irregular Adverbs	Susan plays tennis **better than** John. She can also run **farther than** John.	Irregular adverbs have the same form as irregular adjectives.

2   Ben and John are friends. They do a lot of things together. Ben is better than John in many things. Write sentences using the cues and the pictures.

Examples: (early) *Ben finishes earlier than John (does).*
          (late) *John finishes later than Ben (does).*

plays

swims

1.

a.   (hard) _____

b.   (good) _____

c.   (bad) _____

2.

a.   (fast) _____

b.   (slow) _____

c.   (quick) _____

skis

runs

3.

a.   (dangerous) _____

b.   (safe) _____

c.   (careful) _____

4.

a.   (far) _____

b.   (hard) _____

c.   (serious) _____

C. Comparisons with (not) As . . . as

As . . . as shows that two people, situations, or things are the same in some way. *Not as . . . as* shows that the first person, situation, or thing is less or smaller in some way than the second.

	Examples
As* + adjective + *as	John is **as intelligent as** Patty. (They are equal.)
Not as* + adjective + *as	He isn't **as intelligent as** Albert. (Albert is more intelligent.)
As* + adverb + *as	John plays chess **as slowly as** Dave. (They are equal.)
Not as* + adverb + *as	John doesn't sing **as well as** he used to. (He used to sing better.)

3 Dave is another one of John's friends. Dave does everything about as well as John. With a partner, fill in the correct forms of the words in parentheses. Then take turns asking and answering the questions. Use *as . . . as* in your answers.

Example: How <u>*far*</u> (far) can Dave run?
Dave can run <u>*as far as John.*</u>

1. How _____ (fast) can Dave run? Dave can run _____.

2. How _____ (good) can Dave run? Dave can run _____.

3. How _____ (careful) does Dave ski? Dave skis _____.

4. How _____ (good) does Dave ski? Dave skis _____.

5. How _____ (dangerous) does Dave ski? Dave skis _____.

6. How _____ (quick) does Dave learn? Dave learns _____.

7. How _____ (clear) does he write? Dave writes _____.

8. How _____ (good) does he speak? Dave speaks _____.

4 Similes are sayings that compare two things. Similes often use *as* + adjective + *as*. Match the words on the left with the expressions on the right. Then make sentences with *as . . . as*. Use members of your class for the subjects.

Example: *Fabio is as stubborn as a mule.*

stubborn	as the hills
happy	as gold
fast	as the wind
good	as a mule
quiet	as a clam
old	as a mouse

5 I'm Susan. I'm married to John Wilson. We got married 20 years ago. He has changed in some ways in 20 years, and I have too. Fill in the correct forms of the words on the left.

1. (handsome) John isn't as <u>*handsome*</u> as he used to be. In other words, he used to be <u>*more handsome.*</u>

2. (lazy) I am not as _____ as I used to be. In other words, I used to be

   _____.

3. (good) John doesn't play basketball as _____ as he used to. In other words, he used to play _____.

4. (bad) He isn't as _____ at cards as he used to be. In other words, he used to be _____.

5. (slow) I don't swim as _____ as I used to. In other words, I used to swim _____.

6. (good) I am not as _____ at other sports as I used to be. In other words, I used to be _____ at sports.

7. (quick) John doesn't run as _____ as he used to. In other words, he used to run _____.

8. (careless) He isn't as _____ as he used to be. In other words, he used to be _____.

6 Complete this reading. Circle the correct forms of the words in parentheses.

You're As (Young)/Younger) As You Feel

Hi! I'm Mel. I'm John's father. I used to work in a factory. I was a welder. My job was

(more hard / hardly / harder) than most other jobs, but it was (more interesting /
       1   2

more interested) too. I worked (quickly / quicker / more quickly) and also (careful /
                                    3

carefully / more carefully) than other workers. My work was (good / more good /
     4   5

better) than most of the other welders. Anyway, that doesn't matter now. I am   5

retired.

What do I do with my free time? A lot! Some retired people are (bored / boring).
                                                     6

That's because they have (bored / boring) lives. They sit around the house and
                             7

don't do anything. It's their own fault, if you ask me. It's true, I am not as (young /

younger / more young) as I used to be. So what? My life is never (bored / boring). 10
     8   9

It's easy (find / to find) things to do. I (go / play) cards, I (watch / see) TV, and I
              10   11   12

(go / play) bowling. It's always fun (read / to read), (work / to work) in my garden,
  13   14   15

and (to go / to play) tennis. Oh, yeah. Another thing, I love to travel. How could I
      16

possibly be (bored / boring)? Your life is as (good / well) as you make it.
      17   18

Older people usually like to be independent. Some older people live with their sons and daughters, but most like to live on their own. Another option is a special retirement community—groups of houses or apartments for older people. Usually you have to be more than 60 years old to live in one of these communities.

Using What You've Learned

7 **Writing About Changes.**   How many changes will you feel when you are old? Imagine you are 70 years old. Make at least ten groups of sentences like those in Activity 5. You may use the list of words in Activity 5, but be sure to add some of your own.

8 **Talking About Retirement.**   Discuss these questions.

1. Do you know any people who are retired?
2. Are their lives exciting or boring?
3. Do they enjoy life more now than when they were working?
4. What do they do with their free time?
5. When you retire, what will your life be like?
6. Will you travel to great destinations?

PART 4 # Superlatives with Adjectives and Adverbs

Setting the Context

Prereading Questions   How old is the woman in the picture? Where is she? What do you think happened to her?

Injured

My name is Esther. I am usually very active, but I had a car accident three weeks ago. I broke my leg. Now I'm going to be in this cast for at least two more months.

How do I entertain myself? I read. I listen to the radio. But for me, the most interesting thing is TV. In fact, TV is so interesting   5
that I often watch it for more than five hours a day.

I watch everything—news, game shows, movies, musical performances, music television, and sports. Then I compare many of the actors, musicians, dancers, and athletes that I see.

Check Your Understanding   Circle T for *True* or F for *False*. Correct the false sentences.

1. T F Esther had a skiing accident.
2. T F She reads five hours a day.
3. T F The most interesting thing for Esther is radio.
4. T F TV is so boring she never watches it.
5. T F She watches many types of shows.

A. Superlatives with Adjectives and Adverbs

Use superlatives to compare three or more people or things. Use *the* with superlatives.

	Examples	Notes
One-Syllable Adjectives and Adverbs	I am **the fastest** runner on our team. Joe runs **the slowest** of anyone.	Add *-est* to one-syllable adjectives and adverbs. Use *the* before the superlative.
Two-Syllable Adjectives Ending in *y*	Jack is **the laziest** person on the team.	Change the *y* to *i*, and add *-est* to two-syllable adjectives ending in *y*.
Longer Adjectives and Adverbs	Watching TV is **the most interesting** thing to do. Esther is **the most dangerous** skier I know. She skis **the most dangerously** of anyone.	Use *the most* with multisyllable adjectives (not ending in *y*). Use *the most* with all multisyllable adverbs.
Irregulars	Janis skis **the best** of anyone I know. She is **the worst** student in our school.	The superlative form of *good* is *best*. The superlative form of *bad* is *worst*.

1   Hi, I'm Esther. Last week I saw these three actors in late-night movies. Use the pictures and your imagination to answer the questions. Use the superlative in your answers.

Vern   Gary   George

Example: Who is the most handsome of the three?

(I think that) Gary is the most handsome (of the three).

1. Who looks the strongest? _____
2. Who looks the most intelligent? _____
3. Who looks the dumbest? _____
4. Who is the most athletic? _____
5. Who is the youngest? _____
6. Who is the heaviest? _____
7. Who is the best actor? _____
8. Who is the worst actor? _____

2   I also saw these three actresses. Use your knowledge and your imagination to answer these questions.

Example: Is Penny more famous than Eva?

No, Eva is more famous than Penny.

Penny   *Eva*   Suzanne

1. Who is the most famous? _____
2. Is Eva prettier than Penny? _____
3. Who is the prettiest? _____
4. Is Penny as old as Suzanne? _____
5. Who is the oldest? _____
6. Is Eva as thin as Suzanne? _____
7. Who is the thinnest?   _____
8. Does Penny look as athletic as Eva? _____
9. Who looks the most athletic? _____
10. Who is the best actress? _____
11. Who is the worst actress? _____

B. Comparatives and Superlatives Used Together

The same sentence can have both the comparative and the superlative. This happens when more than two people or things are compared.

> Julie is **happier than** Joan, but Laura is **the happiest** of the three.
> Ahmad plays football **better than** Harry, but Tony plays **the best.**
> Dave is **more serious than** Kevin, but Bill is **the most serious** of the three.

3   On Sunday, there were three games on TV—a baseball game, a soccer game, and an American football game. Write your opinion of these sports.

Example: (fast) *Football is faster than baseball, but soccer is the fastest of the three.*

1. (slow) _____
2. (interesting) _____
3. (exciting) _____
4. (boring) _____

5. (dangerous) _____

6. (safe) _____

7. (good) _____

8. (popular) _____

4 Last week there was a detective show on TV. It was called "Detective Maggot." The show began with the star (Detective Maggot) speaking. Circle the correct forms in parentheses.

My name is Maggot. I live ((in)/on) Kansas City. I'm a cop. Kansas City is like most

cities. It has (good/well) people, and it has (bad/badly) people. My job is to catch the
        1   2

bad ones. It's a (dirty/dirtier) job, but someone has to do it.
         3

Let me tell you about my last case. It was Monday about noon. I got a call from a

woman. Teresa was her name. . . . No, it was Amanda. That's right, Amanda. I can for- 5

get her name, but I (never could/could never) forget her. Amanda was (frightened/
                                  4   5

frightening). She said her husband (is/was) trying to kill her. I met her at 1:00 P.M. in
                                         6

her hotel lobby.

When I saw her. I was (shocking/shocked). She was (beautiful/more beautiful).
                                   7   8

She was (more/as) beautiful as any movie star. She was (more beautiful/beautifuller) 10
         9   10

than any model. She was (as beautiful/the most beautiful) woman in the world. Hey,
                                    11

what can I say? She was beautiful!

She told me her story. She said her husband (is/was) very powerful. She said he
                                            12

(doesn't/didn't) love her anymore. She said he (is/was) trying to poison her. Then she
   13   14

told me her (husband / husband's) name. It was Ralph Smiley. I almost fell over. He was   15
                                    15

the mayor of our city!

    Late that night, I went to the mayor's house. I entered through a window. I walked

(quick / quickly) toward the living room. When I got there, I couldn't (believe / believed)
        16   17

my eyes. The mayor was (in / on) the floor. There was blood (in / on) the rug. He was
                                        18   19

dead! Next to the body, there was a note.   20

Using What You've Learned

5 **Talking About Sports.**   Work with a partner. Choose three different sports. Make a list of seven adjectives. Then make comparisons like those in Activity 3. Be sure to use both comparatives and superlatives in your sentences.

6 **Talking About Famous People.**   Who are the most famous people you can think of? Choose two people, and write their names in blanks 1 and 2 below. Write the name of a student in your class in the blank 3. Then use the adjectives on page 225 to write comparisons of the three people.

Example: (athletic)
    Tiger Woods is more athletic than Julia Roberts, but Ana is the most athletic of the three.

1. _____   2. _____   3. _____
       famous people   other student

Adjectives

1. (good-looking) _____

   _____

2. (rich) _____

   _____

3. (lazy) _____

   _____

4. (intelligent) _____

   _____

5. (famous) _____

   _____

6. (exciting) _____

   _____

7 **Writing and Telling Stories.**   From Activity 4, you know part of Maggot's story. But there is much more. What did the note say? Who killed Mayor Smiley? Why? Can Detective Maggot find the murderer? With a partner, finish this story with at least seven sentences. Then retell your story to the class. Use both adjectives and adverbs as you retell the story. Also, try to use the following structures at least once: *as . . . as, -er* or *more . . . than, -est,* or *the most.*

Video Activities: Cancun

Before You Watch.

1. The resort city of Cancun is in _____.

   a. Spain   b. Thailand   c. Mexico

2. What activity do people usually **not** do at a beach resort?

   a. visit museums
   b. go swimming
   c. go scuba diving
   d. go sailing

Watch.

1. Most activities in Cancun are on the _____.

   a. water   b. beach   c. island

2.   Check the things that you can do in Cancun:

_____ parasail

_____ scuba dive

_____ take a helicopter ride

_____ ride in a glass-bottom boat

_____ visit Isla Mujeres

_____ go in a submarine

_____ swim with turtles

_____ snorkel

_____ meet famous people

Watch Again.   Complete the sentences with the numbers in the box.

| 10 | 20 | 25 | 2 | 30 | 2 to 3 |

1.   Isla Mujeres is about _____ miles from Cancun. It takes about _____ minutes to get there by boat. The boat ride costs $_____.

2.   You can go parasailing in Cancun. It costs about $_____ to parasail for _____ minutes.

3.   Party boats are not expensive. For about $_____ you can have lunch and go snorkeling.

After You Watch.   Complete the following sentences with the *-ed* or *-ing* form of one of the words below.

interest   fascinate   confuse   entertain   disappoint   excite

1.   Parasailing looks _____.

2.   When I went to Cancun, I couldn't understand anyone. I was very _____.

3.   I love scuba diving. Watching fish swim under the sea is _____.

4.   My brother wants to go to Cancun because he's _____ in scuba diving.

5.   The turtles in Cancun aren't afraid of people. They are very _____.

6.   My trip to Isla Mujeres was cancelled. I was very _____.

Chapter 10

Our Planet

Overview of Past Participles

Setting the Context

Prereading Questions Look at the pictures and describe them. What do these animals have in common?

Life on Our Planet

Life on our planet is incredibly varied. When you think about the varieties of life here, you will be amazed. On October 12, 1999 the world population passed six billion people. More than 1,500 languages and thousands of cultures exist around the world. But we humans are only a part of life on earth. An almost infinite number of plants, animals, insects, and birds also populate our planet.   5

Unfortunately, humans are often destructive to other living things. Consider the following:

- One in four species of mammals* is in danger of extinction.
- One in eight species of birds is in danger of extinction.
- At least 11,046 species of plants and animals face extinction.   10
- Up to 100 species become extinct each day.

Statistics like these frighten us because when a species dies, it will never return. Many people are concerned about protecting all life on earth, and they work hard to stop more damage from happening. However, other people are convinced that our planet is already damaged beyond repair. What do you think?   15

Check Your Understanding

1. What does *extinction* mean?
2. Do you know of any endangered animals or plants? Share some examples.
3. What does *damaged beyond repair* mean?

Mammals warm-blooded animals that produce milk for their babies.

A. Past Participles with Verbs of Emotion

For regular verbs, the past participle is the same as the simple past tense (verb + -ed). We use the past participle of many verbs to describe our emotions or feelings. A variety of prepositions can follow the past participle. See Chapter 9 for more information on other forms of these verbs.

Subject + verb (any tense)	Subject + *be* (any tense) + past participle
The test worries me.	I **am worried** about the test.
The instructions confused me.	I **was confused** by the instructions.
The film will shock you.	You **will be shocked** by the film.

Verbs	Past Participles + Possible Prepositions	Verbs	Past Participles + Possible Prepositions
amaze	amazed (at)	frighten	frightened (by)
bore	bored (with)	frustrate	frustrated (with)
concern	concerned (about)	interest	interested (in)
confuse	confused (about)	please	pleased (with)
convince	convinced (about)	satisfy	satisfied (with)
determine	determined (to)	sadden	saddened (about)
disappoint	disappointed (about)	scare	scared (of)
disgust	disgusted (about)	shock	shocked (about)
excite	excited (about)	surprise	surprised (about)
exhaust	exhausted (from)	tire	tired (of)
		worry	worried (about)

1   Complete the reading by circling the correct words in parentheses.

Working to Protect the Environment

My name is Stella, and I am (concern / (concerned))

about environmental issues. I am (convince / con-
                                              1
vinced) that our planet is in trouble. Many things

(worry / worried) me. Air and water pollution in our
      2

major cities (scare / scared) me. I am (frighten / fright-   5
                    3   4
ened) about changes in our weather. And I am

(sadden / saddened) about the animals and plants
      5

around the world that are (endanger / endangered).
                                            6

Do environmental issues (worry/worried) you? If you are (worry/worried), do
                                    7   8
something about it. Don't just be (concerned/concerning). Try to help! If you are   10
                                    9
(interest/interested), join us today!
   10

2 Rewrite these sentences to use past participles. Be sure to use a preposition.

Example: Environmental issues **worry** many people.

Many people are worried about environmental issues.

1. The large animals in Africa **worry** many people.

   _____

2. Learning about African wildlife **interests** Stella.

   _____

3. Protecting wildlife **concerns** many zoos and nature preserves.

   _____

4. At the zoo, the lion **frightened** the little boy.

   _____

5. Seeing a tiger is going to **excite** the little girl.

   _____

6. Spending the whole day at the zoo **exhausted** the mother.

   _____

7. The small cages for animals in some zoos **shock** people.

   _____

8. Wild animals in circuses **sadden** many adults.

   _____

B. Be and Get + Past Participle

We often use past participles in expressions with *be* and *get*. *Get* has the meaning of
become. Part 3 of this chapter gives more information on the verb *be* with past participles (the passive voice forms of verbs).

Subject + *be* + past participle	Subject + *get* + past participle
I'm bored. Let's go to a movie.	Children often **get bored** on rainy days.
Jack **was confused** about the assignment.	I **got confused** because people were speaking fast.
She **is tired** because she stayed up late.	Because of her illness, she **gets tired** easily.

3 Complete these sentences in your own words. Then, read your sentences to your group.

1. Sometimes I get concerned about _____.

2. My family often gets worried about _____.

3. I often get confused about _____.

4. Sometimes I get disappointed about _____.

5. I really get tired of _____.

6. I am (not) satisfied with _____.

7. I am pleased with _____.

8. I am excited about _____.

9. I am usually bored by _____.

10. My friends are frustrated by _____.

C. Common Expressions with Past Participles

Here are common expressions that use past participles. Some of these verbs are regular, and the past participle has the *-ed* ending. Others are irregular and may change spelling and/or pronunciation. Part 2 gives more information on irregular forms, and Appendix 3 (page 260) gives a list of the most common irregular verbs in English.

Verbs	Past Participles	Examples
arrest	arrested	The criminal was **arrested** by the police.
break	broken	The front window is **broken.**
build	built	That house is very well **built.**
close	closed	The library is **closed** now.
damage	damaged	The table was **damaged,** but now it's fixed.
drink	drunk	The man got **drunk** at the party.
(re)elect	(re)elected	The mayor was **reelected** last month.
endanger	endangered	Many animals are **endangered.**
finish	finished	Is your homework **finished?**
go	gone	There's no more sugar. It's all **gone.**
hurt	hurt	Martin got **hurt** during the soccer game.
know	(well) known	That actor is very well **known.**
involve	involved	He's not **involved** in that project.
lose	lost	I got **lost** on the way to your house.
pollute	polluted	That river is very **polluted.**
shut	shut	Are all the doors **shut?**
upset	upset	She was **upset** about her bad grades.
vary	varied	Her problems are **varied.**
write	(well) written	That paper was very well **written.**

Verbs	Past Participles	Examples
divorce	divorced from	He got **divorced from** his wife in 1984.
engage	engaged to	When did Susan get **engaged to** her boyfriend?
marry	married to	Mary got **married to** Charles in Las Vegas.
separate	separated from	Diane **separated from** her husband last month.

4 This is the beginning of the story of Sam Sleeze. Write the past participles in the blanks in each section.

1. | married   invited   elected   engaged   interested |

In 1980, Sam Sleeze got _engaged_ to his girlfriend, and in 1981, the couple got

_____ in a large wedding in Corrupt Town. All of the important people in
                1

town were _____ to the wedding because Sam was _____ in poli-
                         2   3

tics. He was hoping to get _____ mayor.
                                      4

2. | broken   drunk   hurt   arrested |

At the wedding, there was a lot of alcohol and many

people got _____. One man fell off a chair and
                      1

got _____. Another man's arm was
              2

_____ because he fell off a table. Finally, the
          3

police came and several guests were _____.
                                                  4

3. | interested   upset   disappointed |

During the wedding day, Sam's new wife Sue was _____ and
                                                              1

_____ because Sam did not stay with her and forgot about her. He was
          2

_____ in getting money for his political campaign.
          3

4. | reelected   separated   divorced   finished |

Sam and Sue Sleeze did not have a happy life together, and after Sam's election as

mayor, the couple _____. When Sam's first term as mayor was
                              1

_____ he decided to run for mayor again. When Sam got _____,
          2   3

Sue filed for divorce. They got _____ in 1990.
                                          4

5. | built | polluted | determined | worried |

While he was mayor, Sam became very rich. At the same time, many new factories were _____ in Corrupt Town. Before Sam Sleeze was mayor, Corrupt Town was
　　　　　　　　　1
a quiet, peaceful little town. But everything changed. While Sam was becoming richer, the town was becoming poorer. Citizens were _____. Their air and water were
　　　　　　　　　　　　　　　　　　　　　　　2
_____, and their children weren't healthy. One person, Jack Powers, said, "Enough!"
　　3
Powers was _____ to stop the damage.
　　　　　　　　　4

5 This is the conclusion of the story about Sam Sleeze. Choose the correct past participles to complete this story.

<h3 style="text-align:center">LOCAL HERO SAVES OUR TOWN!</h3>

1. | concerned | disgusted | interested | worried |

Ten years ago, the Sludge Company wanted to build a factory along Crystal River. At that time, everyone in town was _worried_ about pollution in the river, and many people protested against the factory. But our mayor, Sam Sleeze, didn't listen. He wasn't _____ about
　　　　　　　　　　　　　　　　　　　1
pollution. He was really _____ in
　　　　　　　　　　　　　　　2
money and the Sludge Company wanted to give him a large contribution for his reelection campaign. People in town were _____ about this money, but the mayor took it anyway.
　　3

2. | built | frightened | reelected | shocked |

When Mayor Sleeze was _____ and began his second term, he signed a con-
　　　　　　　　　　　　1
tract with the Sludge Company. Soon, the factory was _____, and production
　　　　　　　　　　　　　　　　　　　　　　2

began. Everyone in town got even more _____ about pollution when yellow and pur-
                                          3
ple smoke began coming from the smokestacks, and orange and green chemicals began
flowing into the river. Everyone was _____ by the horrible smells from the factory.
                                        4

3. | arrested   closed   determined   exhausted   upset |

One young lawyer in town, Jack Powers, was very _____
                                                    1
about the whole situation. He was _____ to stop the pollution. He
                                     2
worked on this case to find laws against the mayor and against the factory. He stayed up late each night until he was _____, and finally,
                                                    3
he found a way to close the factory and to arrest Mayor Sleeze for ac-
cepting illegal campaign contributions. Yesterday, the Sludge Company
factory was _____. And last night, Mayor Sleeze was _____
               4   5
by the police while he was trying to get on a plane to Mexico.

6 Use the information from the story in Activities 4 and 5 to complete these sentences.
Use the list of characters and places from the story.

the wedding guests	Sam	the Sludge Company
the police	Sue	Corrupt Town
the people of Corrupt Town	the Crystal River	factories
Jack Powers		

1. _____ and _____ got married, separated, and divorced.

2. _____ got drunk.

3. _____ were worried about the pollution.

4. _____ were built in Corrupt Town.

5. _____ was polluted by the factories.

6. A factory was built on the river by _____.

7. _____ was polluted by that factory.

8. _____ was determined to stop Sam Sleeze.

9. Sam Sleeze was arrested by _____.

7 Look back at the list of past participles on page 231. Write original sentences. Write as
many as possible in five minutes.

Using What You've Learned

8 **Organizing a Campaign.** In small groups, choose one issue everyone in the group is concerned about. It might be the environment, social issues, or politics and corruption, for example. Plan a campaign for improving the situation. Make signs or posters about the issue. Plan two or three short speeches. Finally, launch your campaign. Use the following questions to help you.

1. What problem(s) are you concerned about?
2. What specific things can you do now?
3. What should you plan for the future?
4. What might or will happen if you don't do anything now?
5. How can people get involved to help?

9 **Writing Letters.** Choose an environmental issue you, personally, are very concerned about. Write a letter about it to a local, regional, national, or international leader. First explain the problem and then give suggestions for solutions. Finally, mail your letter!

PART 2

Introduction to the Present Perfect Tense

Setting the Context

Prereading Questions Look at the pictures. What are the people doing in each one?

A Smaller Planet

Our planet has become smaller. Not in size, of course. It hasn't really grown smaller. But our lives have changed because we have discovered new technologies. Technological advances in travel and communications have connected the entire world. Today, we can use the telephone or the Internet to communicate with almost anyone, and we can travel by plane, boat, train, or car to almost anywhere. 5
In the past, far away people and places were impossible to reach quickly, but no longer. Today, even the farthest places are seconds away by telephone and the Internet, and perhaps hours away by plane.

Check Your Understanding

1. Is our world really smaller?
2. Why does it seem smaller? Give some examples from the reading. Then add some examples of your own.

Today people around the world have Internet access and can communicate by e-mail and obtain information quickly. Do you have access to the Internet? When did you first get Internet access? What do you use the Internet for?

A. Past Participles of Regular and Irregular Verbs

Two common uses of the past participle are in perfect tenses and in passive voice verbs. This section introduces the present perfect tense, and Part 3 introduces some passive forms.

For regular verbs, the past participle is the same as the simple past tense (verb + *ed*):

Simple Forms	Simple Past and Past Participles	Simple Forms	Simple Past and Past Participles
call	called	study	studied
happen	happened	travel	traveled
play	played	visit	visited

For irregular verbs, the past participle often changes spelling and/or pronunciation. Here is a partial list of irregular past participles. See page 260 for more irregular verbs.

Simple Forms	Past Participles	Simple Forms	Past Participles
be	been	mean	meant
become	become	pay	paid
begin	begun	put	put
bring	brought	read	read
buy	bought	ride	rode
choose	chosen	run	run
come	come	say	said
do	done	see	seen
feed	fed	send	sent
fight	fought	shoot	shot
find	found	sit	sat
get	gotten	speak	spoken
give	given	spend	spent
had	had	take	taken
hold	held	teach	taught
leave	left	think	thought
make	made	win	won

1   Study the irregular past participles on page 236. Then, without looking at the list, complete the missing forms below.

Simple Forms	Past Participles	Simple Forms	Past participles
_be_	been	pay	____
become	____	put	____
begin	____	____	read
bring	____	start	____
____	chosen	see	____
do	____	____	studied
find	____	____	spoken
____	gotten	take	____
____	learned	____	thought
leave	____	travel	____
make	____	visit	____

B. Present Perfect Tense: Affirmative and Negative Statements

The present perfect tense has several uses. A common use is to talk about actions in the past when we don't say or know the specific time. With the present perfect, no specific past time expression is used. Compare: *She has lived in Boston.* (present perfect) *She lived in Boston last year.* (simple past with a specific time)

Subject + *have or has* + past participle	Subject + *haven't or hasn't* + past participle
Affirmative	**Negative**
I You We They **have worked** there.	I You We They **haven't worked** there.
He She It **has worked** there.	He She It **hasn't worked** there.

2   Look at "A Smaller Planet" on page 235. Underline all uses of the present perfect tense. Which verbs have regular past participles? Which have irregular past participles? Write them here.

Regular Past Participles   Irregular Past Participles

have changed _____   *has become* _____

_____   _____

_____   _____

3   Work with a partner. Make true statements from the following cues. Use the example as a model.

Examples: *I have lived in Boston.*
I haven't lived in Madrid.

1. live
   a. in Los Angeles
   b. in Berlin
   c. in Hong Kong
   d. in Mexico City
   e. in Jakarta

2. study
   a. Spanish
   b. Math
   c. American History
   d. Chemistry
   e. Chinese

3. travel
   a. in Europe
   b. in Africa
   c. in Asia
   d. in Australia
   e. in South America

4. visit
   a. Mexico
   b. Egypt
   c. France
   d. Thailand
   e. Canada

5. try
   a. American hamburgers
   b. skiing
   c. surfing
   d. Japanese food
   e. yoga

4   Complete the following with the past participle. Use the verbs in parentheses.

1. Technology has *changed* (change) our lives.

2. Technology has _____ (help) to make travel faster, easier, and cheaper.

3. Long-distance communication has _____ (become) faster and simpler.

4. Computers have _____ (open) new possibilities for communication.

5. Telephones have _____ (give) us a way to communicate with our friends and families from almost any place on earth.

6. Computer technology has _____ (bring) many improvements in our lives.

7. Hundreds of millions of people have _____ (use) the Internet to communicate.

8. All of this technology has _____ (make) our planet seem much smaller.

5   Have you changed during this course? What have you done? What have you accomplished? Tell about changes in your life. Complete the sentences below with true information.

Example: During this course, I have become *more fluent in English.*

1. During this course, I have spoken _____.
2. During this class, I have become _____.
3. I have met people from _____.

4. I have made friends with _____.
5. During this course, I have tried _____.
6. I have gotten _____.
7. During this class, I have learned how to _____.
8. I have learned about _____.

6 List five things that you have already done today.

1. _____
2. _____
3. _____
4. _____
5. _____

7 List five things that you haven't done today but that you plan to do.

1. _____
2. _____
3. _____
4. _____
5. _____

C. Present Perfect Tense: Questions

Form	*Have/Has* + subject + past participle		
Yes/No Questions	**Short Answers**		
		Affirmative	**Negative**
Have { I / you / we / they } **helped?**		Yes, { I / you / we / they } **have.**	No, { I / you / we / they } **haven't.**
Has { he / she / it } **helped?**		Yes, { he / she / it } **has.**	No, { he / she / it } **hasn't.**

Information Questions	Possible Answers
Who has visited Russia?	Nancy has been there twice.
How has he **helped?**	He has cleaned the entire house!
Where has she **lived?**	She has lived in five countries.
Why have they **moved?**	Because of problems with their neighbors.

8 Tell more about your experiences during this course. In pairs, ask and answer these questions.

Example: Who has helped you the most during this course?
My roommate has helped me very much.

1. Who has helped you the most during this course?
2. What have you learned to do well during this semester or quarter?
3. What new foods have you tried?
4. Who have you become friends with during this course?
5. What new things have you learned about other countries and cultures?
6. What have you learned about studying languages?

9 Continue talking about your experiences. In different pairs, ask and answer these questions. Then, you can choose one question to answer in a short composition.

Example: What is the most unusual thing you have done during this course?
The most unusual thing I have done is scuba diving.

1. What is the most unusual thing you have done this year?
2. What is the hardest thing you have done?
3. Who is the funniest person you have met during this course?
4. What is the best movie you have seen?
5. What is the longest story or book you have read during this course?
6. What is the prettiest place you have visited this year?
7. What is the best food you have tried recently?
8. What is the most interesting thing that you have learned (besides English grammar, of course!)?
9. What is the best song you have heard recently?
10. What is the most dangerous thing you have done?

Using What You've Learned

10 **Telling About Yourself.**   What are the best and the worst parts of your life? What things have you done or accomplished? What has happened to you? Write at least eight statements. Use some of these categories to help you. Then work in small groups and share your experiences. Remember that you do not give a specific time in the past when you use the present perfect tense.

Example: *The best thing that I have done? I have run in a marathon!*

The Best	
The Worst	
The Funniest	
The Most Dangerous	
The Most Difficult	
The Most Embarrassing	

PART 3	# Introduction to the Passive Voice

Setting the Context

Prereading Questions   Look at the photos below. What is happening? Do you know these organizations?

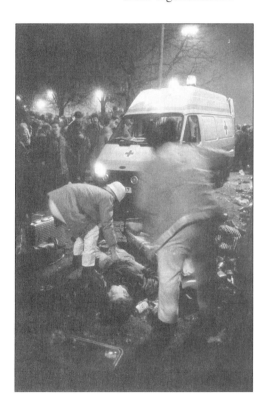

The Red Cross and Red Crescent Societies

The Red Cross flag is seen in many countries around the world. It is respected by citizens, governments, and soldiers. There are many humanitarian organizations, but the Red Cross is the largest in the world. It was founded in 1919. The international headquarters is located in Geneva, Switzerland, and offices are located in 176 different countries. In the Islamic world, the organization is called the Red   5
Crescent. The purpose of the Red Cross and the Red Crescent is to help people who suffer from natural disasters or wars. Help is offered to people without discrimination. Nationality, race, religious beliefs, or political opinions are not considered. Anyone can be helped by the Red Cross or the Red Crescent. The Red Cross and the Red Crescent are nonprofit organizations, so volunteers are always needed.   10

Check Your Understanding

1.   What do you know about the Red Cross where you live?
2.   What other international organizations do you know about?
3.   Have you volunteered in any organizations? Explain.

A. Passive Versus Active Voice

Many verbs in English can use either the active or the passive voice. Compare:
Active: John mailed the letter.
The active voice focuses on the person or thing that *does* the action: *John.*

Passive: The letter was mailed (by John).
The passive voice focuses on the person or thing that *receives* the action: *the letter.*

B. Phrases with by

In some passive sentences, it is important to know *who* did the action. These sentences use *by* + person or thing. In other passive sentences, the result of the action is more important. These sentences do not use *by.* Compare:

Without *by*	With *by*
The letter was mailed.	The letter was mailed **by John, not by Sue.**
The book was written in 1999.	The book was written **by Mary Gill.**
The window was broken last week.	The window was broken **by three teenage boys in blue jeans.**

C. The Passive Voice with Simple Tenses

	Affirmative	Negative
Active Voice	John repaired the car. Mary fixed the phones.	John didn't repair the car. Mary didn't fix the phones.
Passive Voice	Subject + *be* + past participle	Subject + *be* + *not* + past participle
Simple Past	The car **was repaired.** The phones **were fixed.**	The car **wasn't repaired.** The phones **weren't fixed.**
Simple Present	The car **is repaired.** The phones **are fixed.**	The car **isn't repaired.** The phones **aren't fixed.**
Simple Future	The car **will be repaired.** The phones **will be fixed.**	The car **won't be repaired.** The phones **won't be fixed.**

1   Complete the following with the passive form of the verb. Use the simple past, present, or future tense. For a list of the irregular past participles, see Appendix 3, page 260.

Example: pay   The bill ___was paid___ yesterday.

Usually, the bills ___are paid___ at the beginning of the month.

That bill ___will be paid___ tomorrow.

1. finish   The project _____ yesterday.

Their project _____ now.

Gloria's project _____ next week.

2. elect   The next president _____ a month from now.

Jack _____ president of the club last month.

A new president _____ every year.

3. give   Jose _____ the prize last week.

Who _____ the prize next week?

Prizes _____ each week.

4. repair   The TV _____ last week.

The radio _____ now.

The telephone _____ tomorrow.

5. make   That decision _____ at last month's meeting.

In general, decisions _____ at the monthly meeting.

An important decision _____ tomorrow night.

6. not do   The work _____ tomorrow.

The work _____ on Fridays.

The work _____ last night.

7. write   The reports _____ at the end of each month.

My report _____ next week.

The last report _____ late.

8. not understand   His speech last night _____.

Esperanto _____ by most people.

Your presentation _____ tomorrow. Please simplify it.

D. Common Expressions with Regular Verbs

Here are a variety of expressions that use passive voice verbs. Part 1 has additional expressions.

Expressions	Examples
be awarded to	The prize **was awarded to** Martin.
be based on	The movie **was based on** the book.
be cancelled	The game **was cancelled** because of the rain.
be composed of	The team **is composed of** nine players.
be connected to	The video **is connected to** the TV.
be crowded (with)	The theater **was crowded with** children.
be discovered by	Radium **was discovered by** Marie Curie.
be faced with	He **was faced with** a serious problem.
be filled (with)	This paper **is filled with** mistakes.
be invented by	The steam engine **was invented by** James Watt.
be located in (at)	Stanford University **is located in** California.
be related to	Stella **is related to** the president.
be used for (as, by, with)	Scissors **are used for** cutting.
be used to + verb	A hammer **is used to** pound nails.

2   Complete these sentences with verbs in the passive voice. Use the simple past or present tense.

1. Gunpowder ___*was used*___ (use) by the Chinese for fireworks.

2. Gunpowder _____ (introduce) to Europe by the Arabs.

3. The first guns _____ (develop) by the Arabs in the 14th century.

4. Gunpowder _____ (not use) for peaceful purposes, such as mining, until the 17th century.

5. New and powerful explosives _____ (discover) by the Swedish chemist, Alfred Nobel, in the 1860s.

6. For example, dynamite _____ (invent) by Nobel.

7. Nobel _____ (concern) about the destructiveness of his invention.

8. He _____ (interest) in using his money from dynamite to help the world.

9. The Nobel Prizes _____ (create) to help scientists and scholars improve our world.

10. The Nobel Prize awards _____ (start) in 1901.

11. Today, the Nobel Prize committees _____ (locate) in Sweden and Norway.

12. The committees _____ (compose) of Swedish and Norwegian scholars.

13. Most of the Nobel Prizes _____ (award) in October of each year.

14. The prize money _____ (use) for many different purposes.

E. Common Expressions with Irregular Verbs

Verbs	Examples
be born	Alex **was born** in July.
be chosen for (by, to)	Camila **was chosen to** represent the class.
be given to	The prize **was given to** Susan.
be known for (to)	Marina **is known for** her kind personality.
be made from (of)	This shirt **is made of** cotton.
be shown	The first movie **was shown** in Paris.
be written by	*MacBeth* **was written by** Shakespeare.

3 Complete these sentences with verbs in the passive voice. Use the simple past tense. Notice that all verbs are irregular.

1. In 1964, the Nobel Peace Prize _was given_ (give) to Martin Luther King, Jr.

2. King _____ (choose) for the award because of his work for civil rights.

3. King _____ (bear) in the American south in 1929.

4. Most of his life _____ (spend) working for equal rights and equal opportunities for all people.

5. In the 1950s, King _____ (make) a Baptist minister in Montgomery, Alabama, where he worked against racial discrimination.

6. Many of his ideas _____ (take) from Mohandas Gandhi, especially the idea of passive resistance.

7. Boycotts of segregated buses, stores, restaurants, and schools _____ (begin).

8. A protest march on Washington, D.C. _____ (hold) in 1963; during this march, King made one of his most famous speeches.

9. Unfortunately, King's work _____ (leave) unfinished.

10. He _____ (shoot) to death in Memphis, Tennessee, on April 4, 1968.

The U.S. Civil Rights Act of 1964 officially prohibits discrimination in voting, jobs, public accommodations, and so on. However, problems with discrimination continue to exist. What can be done to end discrimination?

4 Complete the following paragraphs with the passive voice form of the simple past, present, or future tense. Use the verbs in parentheses. Pay attention to singular and plural forms of the verb *be*.

World Organizations

The idea of a world organization is not new. After World War I _was fought_ (fight),

from 1914 to 1918, leaders from many countries _____ (determine) to stop

1

wars. The idea of a world organization _____ (discuss) soon after World

2

War I, and the League of Nations _____ (form) in 1920. It

3

_____ (locate) in Geneva, Switzerland. It _____ (mean) to be   5

4   5

a place for leaders of countries to talk to each other to stop future wars.

The League of Nations was not very successful, and it _____ (disband)

6

before World War II. After World War II, another world organization _____

7

(propose). In 1945, the United Nations _____ (begin) in San Francisco.

8

Today, the United Nations headquarters _____ (locate) in New York City.   10

9

Is the United Nations a success or failure today? It _____ (say) that

10

large countries like the United States _____ (give) too much power. It is

11

true that much of the U.N.'s budget _____ (pay) by the United States. Yet

12

the U.N. _____ (make) up of so many countries, over 190, so no country

13

can have complete control. In any case, millions of people around the world   15

_____ (help) by this organization. World problems _____ (dis-

14   15

cuss) and sometimes _____ (solve), children _____ (edu-

16   17

cate), families _____ (feed), and sick people _____ (provide)

18   19

medical care, all through the efforts of the U.N.

How long will the U.N. exist in the future? No one can say. Perhaps it   20

_____ (disband) someday, like the League of Nations. But then, maybe a

20

newer and stronger organization _____ (create) in its place.

21

5 Complete the following story with the simple past tense. Choose the active or the passive voice. Use the verbs in parentheses.

Gandhi, A Model of Nonviolent Action

Mohandas K. Gandhi was one of the most important political activists of all time. He _was born_ (bear) in 1869, and he _____ (die) in 1948. He _____ (live) in Africa and India, but he _____ (know) worldwide for his work. He _____ (become) famous because he _____ (use) nonviolent action. 5

During Gandhi's life, India _____ (control) by Great Britain. Even though many In- 10 dians _____ (want) independence, they _____ (not give) control of their country by the British. Many different ideas _____ (discuss) about how to get independence. Some Indians _____ (buy) guns and _____ (fight) in bloody confrontations, but Gandhi _____ (teach) nonviolent action.

Finally, in 1947, India _____ (give) independence. Gandhi's work 15 _____ (not finish) because the new India _____ (face) with many new problems. But, sadly, Gandhi _____ (kill) in 1948. Gandhi's work _____ (end) with his death, but his ideas and beliefs _____ (remain).

Using What You've Learned

6 **Telling About Historical Figures.** Who is a famous historical person? Choose one person to research as a group. First, find information about his or her life. Then prepare notes. Share the information with your classmates. Use these questions to help you prepare. Make a presentation for the class. Each person in your group should speak.

1. Who was the person?
2. When and where was the person born?
3. What was the person known for? Why was she or he important?
4. What examples can you give of this person's work or accomplishments?
5. How do people feel about this person today?
6. What are two questions that you would like to ask that person if she or he were alive?
7. Why did your group choose this person?

PART 4   Review

Setting the Context

Prereading Questions   Look at the photos and describe them. What are some of the challenges our planet is faced with in the 21st century?

The Challenges of the 21st Century

The 20th century brought tremendous changes to our planet. Some of these changes made life on earth much better, but other changes did not. What will the 21st century be like? Will the 21st century bring peace and prosperity for everyone? Or will it bring suffering and destruction? What will life be like for those who come after us? What can we do today to help ensure a good future on this planet for our children and our grandchildren?   5

Check Your Understanding Reread the questions at the end of the passage and give your own answers. What is your opinion?

1 Complete this conversation with the correct forms of the verbs in parentheses. Use simple present, present continuous, or future tense (active voice).

Roberto: Sometimes I _hate_ (hate) to read the newspapers. The news _____

(be often) very depressing.

Juan: Well, that _____ (not be) always true. Look at the article I

_____ (read) right now, "Hope for Peace in the World." Some government

leaders _____ (think) that things _____ (get) better now. They

_____ (believe) that there _____ (be) a better future.

Roberto: I _____ (not know). One person _____ (say) peace

_____ (be) possible, but another person _____ (talk) about more

fighting. Economic news _____ (not look) good either. Some people

_____ (make) so much money while others _____ (have) so little.

Juan: I guess it all depends on your view of the world. But I _____ (hope)

that my view is right.

2 Complete this passage with the correct forms of the verbs in parentheses. Use simple present, present continuous, simple past, or present perfect tense (active voice). In some cases, more than one tense is possible.

The Challenges We Face

Think about life 100 years ago, and then think about life today. So much _has changed_

(change)! Yet, even though life _____ (improve) for millions of people dur-

ing the 20th century, many serious problems and challenges _____ (face)

us today. During the past 100 years, the population of the world _____ (in-

crease) dramatically, and many social, economic, and environmental problems   5

_____ (develop). In 1900, the world population _____ (be)

about 1.6 billion. By 1990, it _____ (be) more than five billion.

Today, our population is _____ (grow) more rapidly than at any time in
history. As a result, every day there _____ (be) more and more people,
and each person _____ (need) food, clothing, health care, education,   10
housing, and a healthy environment. Every person on earth _____ (want)
a happy and healthy life. What can we and our leaders do to ensure this?

3   Think about the world today. Then complete these sentences. Use your own ideas and opinions. Then share your answers in a group.

1.   World leaders should _____.

2.   Every citizen of the world should _____.

3.   One hundred years ago, people in some parts of the world couldn't _____.

4.   In the future, the United Nations might _____.

5.   Government leaders don't have to _____.

6.   Government leaders must not _____.

7.   Of course, every person in the world would like to _____.

8.   Every country can _____.

9.   In the future this country will _____.

10.   I would rather _____.

4   Put the words in the sentences in the correct order.

Example: for our planet / take responsibility / all people should
            All people should take responsibility for our planet.

1.   to eat better / need / many people
2.   who / the hungry people / feed / can / ?
3.   most of us / to bed hungry / don't go
4.   some organizations / to hungry people / give food
5.   to find jobs / for people / other organizations / prefer
6.   all poor people / to help / we / should continue
7.   will always / the world / problems / have
8.   better solutions / might / find / we

5   Make questions from these sentences. The underlined words are the answers to your questions.

Example: Martin Luther King, Jr., was born in Atlanta, Georgia.
            Where was Martin Luther King, Jr., born?

1.   Martin Luther King, Jr., worked for equal rights for all people.

2.   Two hundred thousand people marched in Washington, D.C., in 1963.

3.   Martin Luther King, Jr., made a famous speech in 1963.

4. Some people hated him <u>because they were racists</u>.

5. Today more people in America have <u>better opportunities</u>.

6. No, <u>not all people have equal opportunity</u>.

7. Many people have to live <u>on the streets</u>.

8. <u>Maybe, in the future</u>, all people in the world will have equal rights.

6 Each of these sentences has one error. Find the error and correct it.

1. There ~~is~~ *are* a lot of problems in the world.
2. There are much good things in the world.
3. We want find solutions for world problems.
4. Some environmental problems has become very serious.
5. We are worry about pollution.
6. Water pollution is serious problem in many places.
7. Every human is needing clean water to drink.
8. Air pollution is damage historical buildings around the world.
9. Many animals and plants are endangering and might become extinct.
10. Farmers have taking land from wild animals.
11. Hunters often kill elephants for the ivory from its tusks.
12. Elephants are some of the most largest animals on earth.
13. Many environmental problems happen because need jobs and money.
14. How we can solve these problems?
15. We must to try to solve them.

Using What You've Learned

7 **Talking About the Future.**   What will be the big problems in the next 50 years? Make a list of five. What will be the big improvements? Make a list of five. Share your lists with other groups.

Problems

1. _____
2. _____
3. _____
4. _____
5. _____

Improvements

1. _____
2. _____

3. _____

4. _____

5. _____

8 **Talking About Your Own Future.**   You are finishing your English class. What will you do now? What plans do you have for the future? Take some time to tell one another about your future plans.

9 **Describing Your Progress in English.**   Talk with a partner about the progress you have made during this course. Use these questions to help you.

1. Are you pleased with your work during this course?

2. Did you get disappointed or frustrated at times? When and why?

3. Have you understood all the grammatical structures that you have studied? Are you confused about any particular structures?

4. Do you ever get bored with English grammar? (Of course not!) Are you going to take another grammar course?

5. Do you have any final comments about your class or your work?

Checking Your Progress

Check your progress with structures from Chapters 9 and 10. Be sure to review any problem areas.

Part 1.   Choose the correct word(s) to complete each sentence.

1. Jorge _____ in Argentina.
    a. was born
    b. is born
    c. was bear
    d. born

2. The movie was _____.
    a. very boring
    b. bored
    c. very bored
    d. very bore

3. Jim is _____ photography.
    a. interesting
    b. interesting in
    c. interest
    d. interested in

4. The United Nations _____ in 1945.
    a. begun
    b. were begun
    c. beginning
    d. was begun

5. Abdul _____ chemistry.
    a. have studied
    b. has study
    c. has studied
    d. have studying

6. She _____ Madrid.
    a. has visit
    b. has visited
    c. has visiting
    d. is visited

7. John is _____ than Bjorn.
    a. as handsome
    b. handsomer
    c. more handsome
    d. handsome

8. Chris _____ the President.
    a. are related to
    b. is related to
    c. is related of
    d. are related of

9. This book is _____ that one.
   a. more shorter than
   b. shorter
   c. shorter than
   d. more short

10. Paul _____ for his skill at sports.
   a. is know
   b. is known
   c. known
   d. is knowing

11. An answer _____ until tomorrow.
   a. won't be giving
   b. won't be gave
   c. won't be given
   d. won't give

12. Edgar doesn't sing _____ Simon.
   a. as good as
   b. as well as
   c. as best as
   d. better as

13. Why are you _____ the exam?
   a. worried for
   b. worried about
   c. worried on
   d. worried in

14. Who can speak _____ the teacher?
   a. as quick as
   b. as quickly as
   c. quickly than
   d. quick as

15. When _____?
   a. will be finished this book
   b. will finish this book
   c. will this book be finishing
   d. will this book be finished

Part 2.   Circle the correct words to complete this story. Circle ✕ to show that nothing is necessary.

Beginning a new language isn't easy, and sometimes it's very (frustrating/frustrated).
1

Many beginning students get (boring/bored), and most get very (tire/tired)
2   3

after listening to and speaking another language. Some people get completely

(exhaust/exhausted). This is because you have to pay (X/more) closer attention in a
4   5

second language, or you might not understand. But later, when you become (more   5

fluent/fluenter), everything becomes (more easy/easier). Language learning is worth
6   7

the effort, though. It is (say/said), "One language, one man; two languages, two men."
8

When you have (learned/learn) a new language, you become a different person. You
9

can look at life in more (as/than) one way.
10

Video Activities: Recycling

Before You Watch.

1. What are these things usually made of? Write *P* for paper, *A* for aluminum, *G* for glass, or *PL* for plastic. More than one answer may be correct.

_____ soda cans   _____ magazines

_____ shampoo bottles   _____ wine bottles

_____ cereal boxes   _____ light bulbs

2. What is the best way to get rid of trash?

    a. Burn it.   b. Bury it.   c. Recycle it.

Watch.

1. Edco is a company that _____.

    a. buys trash

    b. makes trash

    c. recycles trash

2. Check the kinds of trash that you see.

    _____ milk bottles   _____ bones   _____ clothes

    _____ dishes   _____ newspapers   _____ cans

Watch Again.

1. Number the steps in the recycling process.

    _____ Workers sort the trash into piles.

    _____ Edco sends recycled material to customers.

    _____ Workers collect the trash.

    _____ Large trucks dump the trash at Edco.

After You Watch.   Look at the steps in the process above. Rewrite them in the passive voice.

1. _____

   _____

2. _____

   _____

3. _____

   _____

4. _____

   _____

Appendices

Appendix 1

Parts of Speech, Sentence Parts/Word Order Chart, and Grammar Terms

Parts of Speech

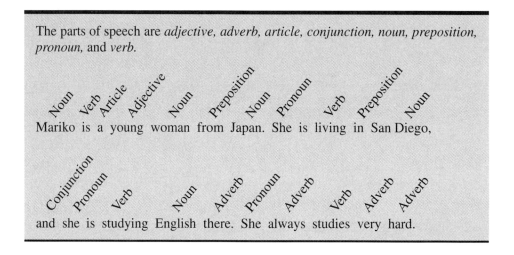

The parts of speech are *adjective, adverb, article, conjunction, noun, preposition, pronoun,* and *verb*.

| Noun | Verb | Article | Adjective | Noun | Preposition | Noun | Pronoun | Verb | Preposition | Noun |

Mariko is a young woman from Japan. She is living in San Diego,

| Conjunction | Pronoun | Verb | Noun | Adverb | Pronoun | Adverb | Verb | Adverb | Adverb |

and she is studying English there. She always studies very hard.

Sentence Parts/Word Order Chart

Subject	Verb	Phrase	Subject	Verb	Object
Mariko	is	from Japan.	Mariko	studies	English.
Mariko	studies	every night.	She	always does	her homework.

Grammar Terms

Term	Definition	Example
Singular	= one	a boy one dog
Plural	= two or more	boys three dogs
Subject	= the main person, place, thing, or idea in a sentence	**Mariko** came yesterday. **She** is from Japan. **Her mother** is going to visit her soon.
Verb	= an action or situation	Mariko **came** yesterday. She **is** from Japan.
Object	= the receiver of an action	Mariko met **her mother** at the airport. Mariko bought **a present** for her mother.
Phrase	= two or more words together	yesterday afternoon from Japan in the United States
Sentence	= a subject/verb combination that expresses a complete idea	Mariko came yesterday afternoon. She is from Japan. She is living in the United States. (*not:* She from Japan. She in the United States.)

Appendix 2

Numbers and Calendar Information

Numbers

This chart gives you both the cardinal and the ordinal numbers. Note that the thirties, forties, and so on, follow the same pattern as the twenties.

Cardinal	Ordinal	Cardinal	Ordinal
zero		twenty	twentieth
one	first	twenty-one	twenty-first
two	second	twenty-two	twenty-second
three	third	twenty-three	twenty-third
four	fourth	twenty-four	twenty-fourth
five	fifth	twenty-five	twenty-fifth
six	sixth	twenty-six	twenty-sixth
seven	seventh	twenty-seven	twenty-seventh
eight	eighth	twenty-eight	twenty-eighth
nine	ninth	twenty-nine	twenty-ninth
ten	tenth	thirty	thirtieth
eleven	eleventh	forty	fortieth
twelve	twelfth	fifty	fiftieth
thirteen	thirteenth	sixty	sixtieth
fourteen	fourteenth	seventy	seventieth
fifteen	fifteenth	eighty	eightieth
sixteen	sixteenth	ninety	ninetieth
seventeen	seventeenth	(one) hundred	(one) hundredth
eighteen	eighteenth	(one) thousand	(one) thousandth
nineteen	nineteenth	(one) million	(one) millionth

Calendar Information

Days of the Week		Months of the Year		Seasons
Sunday	Sun.	January	Jan.	Winter
Monday	Mon.	February	Feb.	Spring
Tuesday	Tues.	March	Mar.	Summer
Wednesday	Wed.	April	Apr.	Autumn or Fall
Thursday	Thurs.	May		
Friday	Fri.	June		
Saturday	Sat.	July		
		August	Aug.	
		September	Sept.	
		October	Oct.	
		November	Nov.	
		December	Dec.	

Appendix 3

Irregular Verbs

Simple Form	Past	Past Participle	Simple Form	Past	Past Participle
be	was/were	been	leave	left	left
bear	bore	born	lend	lent	lent
become	became	become	lose	lost	lost
begin	begun	begun	make	made	made
bite	bit	bitten	mean	meant	meant
blow	blew	blown	meet	met	met
break	broke	broken	pay	paid	paid
bring	brought	brought	put	put	put
build	built	built	read	read	read
buy	bought	bought	ride	rode	ridden
catch	caught	caught	ring	rang	rung
choose	chose	chosen	run	run	run
come	came	come	say	said	said
cost	cost	cost	see	saw	seen
do	did	done	sell	sold	sold
draw	drew	drawn	send	sent	sent
drink	drank	drunk	shake	shook	shaken
drive	drove	driven	shoot	shot	shot
eat	ate	eaten	shut	shut	shut
fall	fell	fallen	sing	sang	sung
feed	fed	fed	sit	sat	sat
feel	felt	felt	sleep	slept	slept
fight	fought	fought	speak	spoke	spoken
find	found	found	spend	spent	spent
fly	flew	flown	stand	stood	stood
forget	forgot	forgotten	steal	stole	stolen
freeze	froze	frozen	sweep	swept	swept
get	got	gotten	swim	swam	swum
give	gave	given	take	took	taken
go	went	gone	teach	taught	taught
grow	grew	grown	tear	tore	torn
hang	hung	hung	tell	told	told
have	had	had	think	thought	thought
hear	heard	heard	throw	threw	thrown
hit	hit	hit	understand	understood	understood
hold	held	held	win	won	won
hurt	hurt	hurt	write	wrote	written
keep	kept	kept			
know	knew	known			

Appendix 4

Spelling Rules and Irregular Noun Plurals
Spelling Rules for -s, -ed, -er, -est, and -ing Endings

This chart summarizes the basic spelling rules for endings with verbs, nouns, adjectives, and adverbs.

Rule	Word	-s	-ed	-er	-est	-ing
For most words, simply add -s, -ed, -er, -est, or -ing without making any other changes.	clean cool	cleans cools	cleaned cooled	cleaner cooler	cleanest coolest	cleaning cooling

Spelling changes occur with the following.

Rule	Word	-s	-ed	-er	-est	-ing
For words ending in a consonant +y, change the y to i before adding -s, -ed, -er, or -est. Do *not* change or drop the y before adding -ing.	carry happy lonely study worry	carries studies worries	carried studied worried	carrier happier lonelier worrier	 happiest loneliest	 carrying studying worrying
For most words ending in e, drop the e before adding -ed, -er, -est, or -ing. *Exceptions:*	dance late nice save write agree canoe		danced saved	dancer later nicer saver writer	 latest nicest	dancing saving writing agreeing canoeing
For many words ending in one vowel and one consonant, double the final consonant before adding -ed, -er, -est, or -ing. These include one syllable words and words with stress on the final syllable.	begin hot mad plan occur refer run shop win		 planned occurred referred shopped	beginner hotter madder planner runner shopper winner	 hottest maddest	beginning planning occurring referring running shopping winning

Rule	Word	-s	-ed	-er	-est	-ing
In words ending in one vowel and one consonant, do *not* double the final consonant if the last syllable is not stressed. *Exceptions:* including words ending in *w, x,* or *y*	enter happen open travel visit bus fix play sew	buses	entered happened opened traveled visited bused fixed played sewed	opener traveler fixer player sewer		entering happening opening traveling visiting busing fixing playing sewing
For most words ending in *f* or *lf,* change the *f* to *v* and add *-es.* *Exceptions:*	half loaf shelf belief chief proof roof safe	halves loaves shelves beliefs chiefs proofs roofs safes	halved shelved	shelver		halving shelving
For words ending in *ch, sh, s, x, z,* and sometimes *o,* and *-es.* *Exceptions:*	church wash class fix quiz tomato zero dynamo ghetto monarch piano portfolio radio studio	churches washes classes fixes quizzes tomatoes zeroes dynamos ghettos monarchs pianos portfolios radios studios				

Irregular Noun Plurals

person	people	foot	feet	deer	deer	series	series
child	children	tooth	teeth	fish	fish	species	species
man	men			goose	geese		
woman	women			ox	oxen		

Appendix 5

Pronunciation Guidelines for -s and -ed *Endings*

-s Endings: The *-s* ending of verbs and nouns is pronounced in three different ways: *-s, -z,* and *-iz.* Practice the words below, paying attention to the pronunciation of the endings.

-s	-z	-iz
hops	begins	boxes
picks	goes	buzzes
starts	needs	kisses
	studies	washes
	travels	watches

-ed Endings: The *-ed* ending of verbs is pronounced in three different ways: *-t, -d,* and *-id.* Practice the words below, paying attention to the pronunciation of the endings.

-t	-d	-id
helped	carried	needed
looked	climbed	persisted
watched	robbed	waited
zipped	traveled	wanted

Appendix 6

Statement and Question Formation

The simple present and past tenses and have *as a main verb**

	Question Word	Auxiliary Verb	Subject	Auxiliary Verb (and Negative)	Main Verb	Auxiliary Verb	Pronoun
Affirmative Statements			You (I, we, they)		study.		
			Ted (he, she, it)		studies.		
			She (we, they, etc.)		studied.		
Negative Statements			You	don't (didn't)	study.		
			Ted	doesn't (didn't)	study.		
Tag Questions			You		study,	don't	you?
			You	don't	study,	do	you?
			Ted		studies,	doesn't	he?
			Ted	doesn't	study,	does	he?
Yes/No Questions		Do(n't)	you		study?		
		Does(n't)	Ted		study?		
		Did(n't)	she		study?		
Short Responses			Yes, I do (did).	No, I don't (didn't).			
			Yes, he does (did).	No, he doesn't (didn't).			
Information Questions	Where	do	you		study?		
	When	does	Ted		study?		
	Who				studied?		

*Have as a main verb forms statements and questions in the same way as other simple present and past tense verbs.

The continuous and perfect tenses, the modal auxiliaries, and be *as a main verb**

	Question Word	Auxiliary Verb	Subject	Auxiliary Verb (and Negative)	Main Verb	Auxiliary Verb	Pronoun
Affirmative and Negative Statements			Ted	is (was) (not)	studying.		
			Ted	should (may, etc.) (not)	study		
			Ted	has (had) (not)	studied.		
Tag Questions			Ted	is	studying,	isn't	he?
			Ted	isn't	studying,	is	he?
			Ted	should	study,	shouldn't	he?
			Ted	shouldn't	study,	should	he?
			Ted	has	studied,	hasn't	he?
			Ted	hasn't	studied,	has	he?
Yes/No Questions		Is(n't)	Ted		studying?		
		Should(n't)	Ted		study?		
		Has(n't)	Ted		studied?		
Short Responses			Yes, he is.	No, he isn't.			
			Yes, he should.	No, he shouldn't.			
			Yes, he has.	No, he hasn't.			
Information Questions	Where	is	Ted		studying?		
	What	should	Ted		study?		
	How long	has	Ted		studied?		
	Who			is	studying?		

*Be as a main verb forms statements and questions in the same way *as* the auxiliary *be* does.

Appendix 7

Comparative and Superlative Forms of Adjectives and Adverbs

Rules	Positives	Comparatives	Superlatives
Add *-er* and *-est* to: one-syllable adjectives	nice	nicer	the nicest
	young	younger	the youngest
adjectives and adverbs that have the same form	early	earlier	the earliest
	fast	faster	the fastest
	hard	harder	the hardest
	late	later	the latest
Add *-er* and *-est* or use *more, less, the most, the least* with two-syllable Adjectives	funny*	funnier	the funniest
		more funny	the most funny
	shallow	shallower	the shallowest
		more shallow	the most shallow
	slender	slenderer	the slenderest
		more slender	the most slender
Use *more, less, the most, the least* with longer adjectives and most *-ly* adverbs	difficult	more difficult	the most difficult
	interesting	more interesting	the most interesting
	quickly	more quickly	the most quickly
	slowly	more slowly	the most slowly

*With words ending in *-y*, the *-er* and *-est* forms are more common, although both forms are used.

Irregular Adjectives and Adverbs

Adjectives	Adverbs		
bad	badly	worse	the worst
good	—	better	the best
well	well	better	the best
far	far	farther	the farthest
—	—	further	the furthest
little	—	less	the least
many	—	more	the most
much	much	more	the most

Index